The
Basics
of
Astrology

by
Ove H. Sehested

VOLUME III
Tables & Reference Tables

ISBN 0-9601080-3-3

Library of Congress Catalog Card Number: 73-90440

FIRST PRINTING . . . . January 1973
SECOND PRINTING . . . . December 1973
THIRD PRINTING . . . . May 1974
FOURTH PRINTING . . . . . . November 1974
FIFTH PRINTING . . . . February 1976
SIXTH PRINTING . . . . October 1976

URANUS PUBLISHING CO.
5050 Calatrana Dr.
Woodland Hills, CA 91364

PRINTED IN THE U.S.A.

v

CONTENTS OF
APPENDIX

ACKNOWLEDGMENT

The Church of Light is a worldwide organization, headquartered in Los Angeles, California; it is the source of the widely used "hermetic" system of astrology. The Church of Light is not a church in the usual sense, rather it is a repository of a broad range of esoteric teaching—the Religion of the Stars—of which astrology is only one cornerstone.

While astrology is in general a universal body of knowledge, certain details of fact and procedure exclusive to the Church of Light have been presented in this book. These include: The system of orbs of aspects, keywords for the orbs and aspects, exaltations of the planets, mutual receptions (where based on these exaltations), the upper octave concept of the three outer planets, the names of the house groupings, and a discussion of astrodynes.

Some minor changes were instituted in some of the above: for example, the term *abstract,* for the fourth group of houses, was substituted for the hermetic term *psychic,* and the keyword for the opposition aspect, *conflict,* was used instead of the hermetic term *separation.* Since the astrology presented here is *out of context* with the general hermetic course, it was felt that these substitutions provided a little more clarity for the beginning student.

The author wishes to thank the board of directors of the Church of Light for permission to use the above material.

FEEDBACK

Feedback is the sensing system that tells the main mechanism whether or not it is performing its function properly. Missiles use it to stay on course; a rolling mill uses it to maintain the thickness of sheet metal to a fine degree— and so on.

People use it too. If you want to walk across the room, various senses feed back information to the control center of the brain, and that keeps you from bumping into things or falling on your face.

We'd like to put it to use with this book. You, the reader, can provide invaluable feedback that will help us in future editions of holding true to the goal of providing the clearest, most comprehensive, most rewarding textbook on astrology possible.

After you've gone through the book, tell us what you think. Did you have any difficulties, was there any area that was insufficiently covered? And, equally important, what did you like about it?

Please share your thoughts with us. Drop us a line—the address is in the Book Shop section. It would be most appreciated.

LIST OF FIGURES IN THE TEXT.

NEW MOON—May 24d, 0h. 32m. p.m.

10										MAY, 1971			[RAPHAEL'S

D	Neptune		Herschel		Saturn		Jupiter		Mars		
M	Lat.	Dec.	Lat.	Dec.	Lat.	Dec.	Lat.	Dec.	Lat.	Dec.	
	° ′	° ′	° ′	° ′	° ′	° ′	° ′	° ′	° ′	° ′	° ′
1	1N43	18 S 56	0N43	3 S 26	1 S 54	16 N 54	1 N 1	19 S 59	1 S 25	21 S 48	21 S 43
3	1 43	18 56	0 43	3 24	1 54	16 58	1 1	19 57	1 29	21 39	21 35
5	1 43	18 55	0 43	3 23	1 54	17 2	1 1	19 54	1 34	21 30	21 26
7	1 43	18 54	0 43	3 21	1 54	17 5	1 1	19 52	1 39	21 21	21 17
9	1 43	18 54	0 43	3 20	1 54	17 9	1 1	19 49	1 44	21 12	21 8
11	1 43	18 53	0 43	3 19	1 54	17 13	1 1	19 47	1 49	21 3	20 59
13	1 43	18 53	0 43	3 17	1 53	17 17	1 1	19 44	1 54	20 54	20 50
15	1 43	18 52	0 43	3 16	1 53	17 21	1 1	19 41	2 0	20 45	20 41
17	1 43	18 51	0 42	3 15	1 53	17 24	1 1	19 39	2 5	20 36	20 32
19	1 43	18 51	0 42	3 14	1 53	17 28	1 0	19 36	2 11	20 27	20 23
21	1 43	18 50	0 42	3 13	1 53	17 32	1 0	19 33	2 16	20 19	20 14
23	1 43	18 49	0 42	3 12	1 53	17 35	1 0	19 30	2 22	20 10	20 6
25	1 43	18 49	0 42	3 11	1 53	17 39	1 0	19 27	2 28	20 2	19 57
27	1 43	18 48	0 42	3 10	1 53	17 43	1 0	19 24	2 35	19 53	19 49
29	1 43	18 47	0 42	3 9	1 53	17 46	0 59	19 21	2 41	19 46	19 S 42
31	1N43	18 S 47	0N42	3 8	1 S 53	17 N 50	0 N 59	19 S 18	2 S 48	19 S 38	

D	D	Sidereal	☉		☉		☽		☽	☽		MIDNIGHT	
M	W	Time	Long.		Dec.		Long.		Lat.	Dec.		☽ Long.	☽ Dec.
		H. M. S.	° ′ ″		° ′		° ′ ″		° ′	° ′		° ′ ″	° ′
1	S	2 35 3	10♉ 28 13		14N58		1♌14 58		1N37	21N28		7♌24 35	19N29
2	☉	2 39 0	11 26 26		15 16		13 29 56		0N34	17 19		19 31 43	15 0
3	M	2 42 56	12 24 38		15 34		25 30 35		0 S 30	12 33		1♍27 14	10 1
4	Tu	2 46 53	13 22 47		15 52		7♍22 20		1 31	7 24		13 16 31	4N43
5	W	2 50 50	14 20 55		16 9		19 10 22		2 28	2N 1		25 4 28	0 S 43
6	Th	2 54 46	15 19 0		16 26		0≏59 19		3 19	3 S 26		6≏55 22	6 8
7	F	2 58 43	16 17 4		16 43		12 53 2		4 1	8 47		18 52 39	11 23
8	S	3 2 39	17 15 6		16 59		24 54 31		4 33	13 53		0♏58 52	16 16
9	☉	3 6 36	18 13 6		17 16		7♏ 5 51		4 53	18 30		13 15 37	20 33
10	M	3 10 32	19 11 5		17 31		19 28 14		5 0	22 24		25 43 44	24 1
11	Tu	3 14 29	20 9 2		17 47		2♐ 2 7		4 52	25 20		8♐23 23	26 21
12	W	3 18 25	21 6 58		18 3		14 47 31		4 30	27 2		21 14 28	27 22
13	Th	3 22 22	22 4 52		18 18		27 44 15		3 53	27 19		4♑16 50	26 52
14	F	3 26 19	23 2 45		18 32		10♑52 17		3 4	26 3		17 30 36	24 51
15	S	3 30 15	24 0 36		18 47		24 11 55		2 3	23 18		0≈≈56 17	21 25
16	☉	3 34 12	24 58 27		19 1		7≈≈43 51		0 S 55	19 14		14 34 42	16 46
17	M	3 38 8	25 56 16		19 15		21 28 59		0 N 17	14 4		28 26 45	11 11
18	Tu	3 42 5	26 54 4		19 28		5✶28 4		1 30	8 7		12✶32 52	4 S 56
19	W	3 46 1	27 51 50		19 41		19 41 4		2 38	1 S 40		26 52 25	1 N 39
20	Th	3 49 58	28 49 36		19 54		4♈ 6 35		3 37	4 N 57		11♈23 7	8 13
21	F	3 53 54	29♉ 47 21		20 7		18 41 24		4 23	11 23		26 0 43	14 23
22	S	3 57 51	0♊45 4		20 19		3♉ 20 16		4 52	17 12		10♉ 39 8	19 45
23	☉	4 1 48	1 42 47		20 31		17 56 23		5 1	22 0		25 11 7	23 53
24	M	4 5 44	2 40 28		20 42		2♊22 25		4 51	25 24		9♊29 28	26 29
25	Tu	4 9 41	3 38 8		20 53		16 31 36		4 24	27 8		23 28 13	27 21
26	W	4 13 37	4 35 47		21 4		0♋18 57		3 41	27 8		7♋ 3 31	26 30
27	Th	4 17 34	5 33 24		21 14		13 41 51		2 47	25 31		20 13 59	24 11
28	F	4 21 30	6 31 0		21 24		26 40 9		1 46	22 34		3♌ 0 39	20 41
29	S	4 25 27	7 28 35		21 34		9♌15 54		0N41	18 36		15 26 24	16 21
30	☉	4 29 23	8 26 8		21 43		21 32 43		0 S 24	13 57		27 35 28	11 26
31	M	4 33 20	9♊23 39		21N52		3♍35 18		1 S 27	8N50		9♍32 52	6N11

FIRST QUARTER—May 2d, 7h. 35m. a.m.

FULL MOON—May 10d, 11h. 24m. a.m.

| EPHEMERIS] | | | | MAY, 1971 | | | 11 |

D	Venus			Mercury			Node	Mutual Aspects
M	Lat.	Dec.		Lat.	Dec.		)	

	° '	° '	° '	° '	° '	° '	° '	
1	1 S 40	2N 13		1 S 25	7N 45		19≈35	1. ⊙ ▽ ♅. 2. ♀ 8♅.
3	1 41	3 8	2N 41	1 51	7 16	7N 29	19 28	3. ⊙ □ ♇. ☿ Stat. ♀Q ♂.
5	1 42	4 4	3 36	2 15	6 59	7 6	19 22	4. ♀P ♅. 5. ⊙ ∠ ♅, P ♇.
7	1 43	4 59	4 31	2 34	6 51	6 54	19 15	7. ⊙ ± ♅. ♀Q ♀.
9	1 43	5 53	5 26	2 50	6 53	6 51	19 9	8. ♀□ ♃. ♂ ∗ ♀.
			6 20			6 58		9. ⊙P ♄. ♀± ♄.
11	1 43	6 48	7 15	3 2	7 5	7 14	19 3	10. ☿∨ ♄. ♂∗ ♃. ♄ □ ♅.
13	1 42	7 41	8 8	3 12	7 25	7 38	18 56	12. ♀P ♀, ± ♀.
15	1 42	8 35	9 1	3 17	7 53	8 9	18 50	13. ♀∗ ♃. 14. ♀∨♄.
17	1 41	9 27	9 53	3 20	8 28	8 48	18 44	15. ⊙P ♀. ♀± ♃, ± ♀.
19	1 40	10 19	10 45	3 20	9 10	9 33	18 37	16. ⊙ □ ♅. ♀P ♇.
21	1 38	11 10	11 35	3 17	9 57	10 23	18 31	17. ⊙ ♂ ♄. 18. ⊙ △ ♇.
23	1 37	12 0	12 25	3 11	10 50	11 18	18 25	19. ⊙P ♃. ☿∨ ♅. ♀∨ ♃, ∨ ♀.
25	1 35	12 49	13 13	3 3	11 47	12 17	18 18	20. ♀± ♇. ♀∨ ♃, ∨ ♀.
27	1 33	13 37	14 0	2 52	12 48	13 19	18 12	21. ♀± ♅.
29	1 30	14 23	14N 46	2 39	13 51	14N 24	18 6	22. ⊙P ♃. ♃ ♂ ♀.
31	1 S 28	15N 9		2 S 25	14N 58		17≈59	23. ⊙ ♂♃, ♀♀. ♂ △ ♅.
								25. ☿∨ ♅. ♀P ♀.
								26. ♀□ ♂. ♀∨ ♅.
								27. ☿□♇. ♀□ ♂.
								28. ♀± ♅.
								29. ♀± ♅. ♂ □ ♇.
								30. ♀Q ♃.
								31. ⊙ △ ♅. ♀± ♅.

D	♆	♅	♄	♃	♂	♀	☿					Lunar Aspects					
M	Long.	Long.	Long.	Long.	Long.	Long.	Long.	⊙	♇	♆	♅	♄	♃	♂	♀	☿	

	° '	° '	° '	° '	° '	° '	° '										
1	2 ♐ 17	10 ≏ 20	23 ♉ 53	4 ♐ 13	28♐46	9 ♈ 27	23 ♈ 18	∗		△				△	8	
2	2 16	10 18	24 0	4 ♃ 7	29 17	10 39	23 ℞11	□	∠		∗					△
3	2 14	10 16	24 8	4 0	29♐48	11 51	23 9	∨			∠	∠			♍	△
4	2 13	10 14	24 16	3 54	0≈19	13 3	23D 12			□	∨	□		△		♍
5	2 11	10 12	24 23	3 47	0 50	14 16	23 19	△				.	△	.		
6	2 10	10 10	24 31	3 40	1 21	15 28	23 31	♍	♂	∗			♂	♍		∗ △
7	2 8	10 8	24 39	3 33	1 52	16 41	23 48			∠	♂	♍				8
8	2 6	10 6	24 46	3 26	2 22	17 53	24 9	∨						∨		8
9	2 5	10 4	24 54	3 19	2 52	19 5	24 35		∠	∨	∨		∨	∨	♍	
10	2 3	10 2	25 2	3 12	3 22	20 18	25 5	8			∠	8				
11	2 2	10 0	25 9	2 57	5 22	21 30	25 39	∗	♂			△		♂ ∗	♍	
12	2 0	9 59	25 17	2 57	4 21	22 43	26 17			∗						△
13	1 59	9 57	25 25	2 50	4 51	23 55	26 58	□	∨			∨		∨		△
14	1 57	9 55	25 33	2 43	5 20	25 7	27 43	♍	△	∠	□	♍		∠		□ □
15	1 55	9 54	25 41	2 35	5 48	26 20	28 32	△		∨	△	△		△		□ □
16	1 54	9 52	25 48	2 28	6 17	27 32	29 ♈24	□	∗	△		∗		△	●	
17	1 52	9 50	25 56	2 22	6 45	28 45	0 ♉ 20	△		□ □						
18	1 51	9 49	26 4	2 13	7 13	29♈58	1 19		□			∗		∨ ∨	∗ ∗	
19	1 49	9 48	26 12	2 5	7 41	1 ♉ 10	2 20	∗		∠ △	8			△	∨ ∨	
20	1 47	9 46	26 19	1 58	8 9	2 23	3 25	∗	8	△	8			△	∨ ∨	
21	1 46	9 45	26 27	1 50	8 36	3 35	4 33	∠		∠ □		△				
22	1 44	9 43	26 35	1 42	9 3	4 48	5 44		△	∨		∨		♂	♂	
23	1 42	9 42	26 43	1 35	9 30	6 1	6 57	♍	△	♍		□				
24	1 41	9 41	26 50	1 27	9 56	7 13	8 13	♍	△	8		♍	8		∨ ∨	
25	1 39	9 40	26 58	1 19	10 22	8 26	9 32			△					∨ ∨	
26	1 38	9 39	27 6	1 12	10 48	9 38	10 53	∨ □			∨		♍	∗ ∗	
27	1 36	9 37	27 14	1 4	11 13	10 51	12 17			□ □	∨ □	∠		∗ ∗	
28	1 34	9 36	27 21	0 56	11 38	12 4	13 43	∠	∗	△	∗	△		□	
29	1 33	9 35	27 29	0 49	12 3	13 16	15 12	∨	∠	△	∗		8		
30	1 31	9 34	27 37	0 41	12 27	14 29	16 44	∨	∠			∨		∨ ∨	
31	1 ♐ 30	9 ≏ 34	27 ♉ 44	0 ♐ 34	12≈51	15 ♉ 42	18 ♉ 18				∨	∨		∗ ∗	

LAST QUARTER—May 17d, 8h. 16m. p.m.

APPENDIX C
TIME ZONES OF VARIOUS COUNTRIES

PLACE	HOURS
AFGHANISTAN	+ 04:30
ALASKA:	
East of W137^o	− 08:00
West 137° to 141°	− 09:00
West 141° to 161°	− 10:00
West 161° to 172°30'	− 11:00
Aleutian Islands	− 11:00
ALBANIA	+ 01:00
ALGERIA	00:00
ANGOLA	+ 01:00
ARGENTINA	− 04:00
AUSTRALIA:	
Capital Territory	+ 10:00
New South Wales	+ 10:00
(Broken Hill area)	+ 09:30
Northern Territory	+ 09:30
Queensland	+ 10:00
South Australia	+ 09:30
Tasmania	+ 10:00
Victoria	+ 10:00
Western Australia	+ 08:00
AUSTRIA	+ 01:00
AZORES	− 01:00
BAHAMAS	− 05:00
BELGIUM	+ 01:00
BERMUDA	− 04:00
BOLIVIA	− 04:00
BOTSWANA	+ 02:00
BRAZIL:	
Eastern part	− 03:00
Territory of Acre	− 05:00
Western part	− 04:00
BRITISH HONDURAS	− 06:00
BULGARIA	+ 02:00

BURMA	+ 06:30
CAMBODIA	+ 07:00
CAMEROON REPUBLIC	+ 01:00
CANADA:	
Alberta	- 07:00
British Columbia	- 08:00
Labrador	- 03:30
Manitoba	- 06:00
New Brunswick	- 04:00
Newfoundland	- 03:30
Northwest Territory	
East of W68°	- 04:00
West 68° to 85°	- 05:00
West 85° to 102°	- 06:00
West 102° to 120°	- 07:00
West of W120°	- 08:00
Nova Scotia	- 04:00
Ontario	
East of W90°	- 05:00
West of W90°	- 06:00
Quebec	
East of W68°	- 04:00
West of W68°	- 05:00
Saskatchewan	- 07:00
Yukon	- 09:00
CANARY ISLANDS	00:00
CENTRAL AFRICAN REPUBLIC	+ 01:00
CEYLON	+ 05:30
CHAD	+ 01:00
CHILE	- 04:00
CHINA	+ 08:00
COLUMBIA	- 05:00
CONGO REPUBLIC	+ 01:00
CONGOLESE REPUBLIC:	
Eastern part	+ 02:00
Western part	+ 01:00
COSTA RICA	- 06:00
CUBA	- 05:00
CYPRUS	+ 02:00
CZECHOSLOVAKIA	+ 01:00

DAHOMEY	+ 01:00
DENMARK	+ 01:00
DOMINICAN REPUBLIC	- 05:00
ECUADOR	- 05:00
EGYPT	+ 02:00
ESTONIA	+ 03:00
ETHIOPIA	+ 03:00
FIJI	+ 12:00
FINLAND	+ 02:00
FRANCE	+ 01:00
FRENCH GUIANA	- 04:00
GABON	+ 01:00
GAMBIA	00:00
GERMANY	+ 01:00
(East)	+ 01:00)
GHANA	00:00
GIBRALTER	+ 01:00
GREAT BRITAIN	+ 01:00
GREECE	+ 02:00
GUATEMALA	- 06:00
GUINEA REPUBLIC	00:00
GUYANA	- 03:45
HAITI	- 05:00
HONDURAS	- 06:00
HONG KONG	+ 08:00
HUNGARY	+ 01:00
ICELAND	00:00
INDIA	+ 05:30
IRAN	+ 03:30
IRAQ	+ 03:00
IRISH REPUBLIC	+ 01:00
ISRAEL	+ 02:00
ITALY	+ 01:00
IVORY COAST	00:00
JAMAICA	- 05:00
JAPAN	+ 09:00
JORDAN	+ 02:00
KENYA	+ 03:00
KOREA	+ 09:00
KUWAIT	+ 03:00

LAOS	+ 07:00
LATVIA	+ 03:00
LEBANON	+ 02:00
LESOTHO	+ 02:00
LIBERIA	- 00:44
LIBYA	+ 02:00
LIECHTENSTEIN	+ 01:00
LITHUANIA	+ 03:00
LUXEMBURG	+ 01:00
MACAO	+ 08:00
MALAGASY REPUBLIC	+ 03:00
MALAWI	+ 02:00
MALAYSIA:	
Malaya	+ 07:30
Saba, Sarawak	+ 08:00
MALI	00:00
MALTA	+ 01:00
MANCHURIA	+ 09:00
MAURITANIA	00:00
MAURITIUS	+ 04:00
MEXICO	- 06:00
Western States	- 07:00
Northern Baha California	- 08:00
MONACO	+ 01:00
MOROCCO	00:00
NETHERLANDS	+ 01:00
NEW ZEALAND	+ 12:00
NICARAGUA	- 06:00
NIGER	00:00
NIGERIA	+ 01:00
NORWAY	+ 01:00
PAKISTAN:	
East	+ 06:00
West	+ 05:00
PANAMA	- 05:00
PARAGUAY	- 04:00
PERU	- 05:00
PHILIPPINE REPUBLIC	+ 08:00
POLAND	+ 01:00
PORTUGAL	+ 01:00

PUERTO RICO	− 04:00
RHODESIA	+ 02:00
ROMANIA	+ 02:00
SALVADOR	− 06:00
SAMOA	− 11:00
SAUDI ARABIA	+ 03:00
SIERRA LEONE	00:00
SINGAPORE	+ 07:30
SOMALI REPUBLIC	+ 03:00
SOUTH AFRICA	+ 02:00
SOUTH WEST AFRICA	+ 02:00
SPAIN	+ 01:00
SPANISH SAHARA	00:00
SUDAN	+ 02:00
SURINAM	− 03:30
SWAZILAND	+ 02:00
SWEDEN	+ 01:00
SWITZERLAND	+ 01:00
SYRIA	+ 02:00
TAIWAN	+ 08:00
TANGIER	00:00
TANZANIA	+ 03:00
THAILAND	+ 07:00
TOGO	00:00
TRINIDAD	− 04:00
TUNISIA	+ 01:00
TURKEY	+ 02:00
UGANDA	+ 03:00
U S S R:	
West of $E40^{\circ}$	+ 03:00
East 40° to $52^{\circ}30'$	+ 04:00
East $52^{\circ}30'$ to $67^{\circ}30'$	+ 05:00
East $67^{\circ}30'$ to $82^{\circ}30'$	+ 06:00
East $82^{\circ}30'$ to $97^{\circ}30'$	+ 07:00
East $97^{\circ}30'$ to $112^{\circ}30'$	+ 08:00
East $112^{\circ}30'$ to $127^{\circ}30'$	+ 09:00
East $127^{\circ}30'$ to $142^{\circ}30'$	+ 10:00
East $142^{\circ}30'$ to $157^{\circ}30'$	+ 11:00
East $157^{\circ}30'$ to $172^{\circ}30'$	+ 12:00
East of $E172^{\circ}30'$	+ 13:00

UPPER VOLTA	00:00
URUGUAY	- 03:30
VENEZUALA	- 04:00
VIET NAM:	
North	+ 07:00
South	+ 08:00
YUGOSLAVIA	+ 01:00
ZAMBIA	+ 02:00

APPENDIX D
SYSTEMS OF COORDINATES

EARTH	CELESTIAL EQUATOR	ECLIPTIC
Greenwich or Prime Meridian	point of Aries	zero degrees Aries
degrees, minutes, seconds	degrees, minutes, seconds or hours, minutes, and seconds (sidereal)	signs, degrees, minutes
longitude, east or west	right ascension (RA), counter-clockwise, or sidereal hour angle (SHA), clockwise	celestial longitude, counter-clockwise
latitude north or south from the equator	declination north or south (from the celestial equator)	celestial latitude (north or south from the ecliptic)

TABLES OF HOUSES FOR   Latitude 59° 56' N.

Top-left

Sidereal Time (H.M.S.)	10 ♈	11 ♉	12 ♋	Ascen Ω	2 Ω	3 ♍
0 0 0	0 13	2	4	31 18	5	
0 3 40	1 14	3	5	5 18	5	
0 7 20	2 15	4	5	39 19	6	
0 11 0	3 17	5	6	14 20	7	
0 14 41	4 18	5	6	48 20	8	
0 18 21	5 19	6	7	22 21	8	
0 22 2	6 20	7	7	56 22	9	
0 25 42	7 21	8	8	30 22	10	
0 29 23	8 22	9	9	4 23	11	
0 33 4	9 23	9	9	38 23	12	
0 36 45	10 24	10	10	12 24	12	
0 40 26	11 26	11	10	46 25	13	
0 44 8	12 27	12	11	20 25	14	
0 47 50	13 28	12	11	54 26	15	
0 51 32	14 29	13	12	28 27	15	
0 55 14	15 ♊ 11	14	13	2 27	16	
0 58 57	16 1	15	13	36 28	17	
1 2 40	17 2	15	14	10 29	18	
1 6 23	18 3	16	14	45 29	19	
1 10 7	19 4	17	15	19 ♍	19	
1 13 51	20 5	17	15	53 1	20	
1 17 35	21 6	18	16	27 1	21	
1 21 20	22 7	19	17	2 2	22	
1 25 6	23 8	20	17	36 3	23	
1 28 52	24 9	20	18	11 3	23	
1 32 38	25 10	21	18	45 4	24	
1 36 25	26 11	22	19	20 5	25	
1 40 12	27 12	23	19	55 5	26	
1 44 0	28 13	23	20	29 6	27	
1 47 48	29 14	24	21	4 7	27	
1 51 37	30 15	25	21	39 7	28	

Top-middle

Sidereal Time (H.M.S.)	10 ♉	11 ♊	12 ♋	Ascen Ω	2 ♍	3 ♍
1 51 37	0 15	25	21	39 7	28	
1 55 27	1 16	26	22	14 8	29	
1 59 17	2 17	26	22	49 9	♎	
2 3 8	3 18	27	23	25 9	1	
2 6 59	4 19	27	24	0 10	1	
2 10 51	5 20	28	24	36 11	2	
2 14 44	6 21	29	25	11 11	3	
2 18 37	7 22	30	25	47 12	4	
2 22 31	8 23	Ω	26	22 13	5	
2 26 25	9 23	1	26	58 13	6	
2 30 20	10 24	2	27	34 14	6	
2 34 16	11 25	2	28	10 15	7	
2 38 13	12 26	3	28	47 16	8	
2 42 10	13 27	4	29	23 16	9	
2 46 8	14 28	5	29	59 17	10	
2 50 7	15 29	5	0 ♍ 36	18	11	
2 54 7	16 ♋ 6	1	13 18	11	
2 58 7	17 1	7	1	50 19	12	
3 2 8	18 2	8	2	27 20	13	
3 6 9	19 3	8	3	4 20	14	
3 10 12	20 4	9	3	41 21	15	
3 14 15	21 4	10	4	18 22	16	
3 18 19	22 5	10	4	56 23	17	
3 22 23	23 6	11	5	34 23	17	
3 26 29	24 7	12	6	11 24	18	
3 30 35	25 8	12	6	49 25	19	
3 34 41	26 9	13	7	27 26	20	
3 38 40	27 10	14	8	5 26	21	
3 42 57	28 11	15	8	44 27	22	
3 47 6	29 12	15	9	22 28	23	
3 51 15	30 13	16	10	1 28	24	

Top-right

Sidereal Time (H.M.S.)	10 ♊	11 ♋	12 Ω	Ascen ♍	2 ♍	3 ♎
3 51 15	0 13	16	10	1 28	24	
3 55 25	1 14	17	10	39 29	24	
3 59 36	2 14	18	11	18 ♎	25	
4 3 48	3 15	18	11	57 1	26	
4 8 0	4 16	19	12	36 1	27	
4 12 13	5 17	20	13	15 2	28	
4 16 26	6 18	21	13	54 3	29	
4 20 40	7 19	21	14	34 4	♏	
4 24 55	8 20	22	15	13 4	1	
4 29 10	9 21	23	15	53 5	2	
4 33 26	10 22	24	16	32 6	2	
4 37 42	11 23	24	17	12 7	3	
4 41 59	12 23	25	17	52 7	4	
4 46 16	13 24	26	18	32 8	5	
4 50 34	14 25	27	19	12 9	6	
4 54 52	15 26	27	19	52 10	7	
4 59 10	16 27	28	20	32 10	8	
5 3 29	17 28	29	21	12 11	9	
5 7 49	18 29	30	21	53 12	10	
5 12 9	19 Ω	♍ 22	33 13	10	
5 16 29	20 1	1	23	13 14	11	
5 20 49	21 2	2	23	54 14	12	
5 25 9	22 2	3	24	35 15	13	
5 29 30	23 3	3	25	15 16	14	
5 33 51	24 4	4	25	56 17	15	
5 38 12	25 5	5	26	36 17	16	
5 42 34	26 6	6	27	17 18	17	
5 46 55	27 7	6	27	58 19	18	
5 51 17	28 8	7	28	38 20	19	
5 55 38	29 9	8	29	19 20	19	
6 0 0	30 10	10	30	0 21	20	

Bottom-left

Sidereal Time (H.M.S.)	10	11 Ω	12 ♍	Ascen ♎	2 ♎	3 ♏
6 0 0	0 10	9	0	0 21	20	
6 4 22	1 11	10	0	41 22	21	
6 8 43	2 11	10	1	21 23	22	
6 13 5	3 12	11	2	2 24	23	
6 17 26	4 13	12	2	43 24	24	
6 21 48	5 14	13	3	24 25	25	
6 26 9	6 15	13	4	4 26	26	
6 30 30	7 16	14	4	45 27	27	
6 34 51	8 17	15	5	26 27	28	
6 39 11	9 18	16	6	6 28	28	
6 43 31	10 19	16	6	47 29	29	
6 47 51	11 20	17	7	27 30	♐	
6 52 11	12 20	18	8	8 ♏	1	
6 56 31	13 21	19	8	48 1	2	
7 0 50	14 22	20	9	28 2	3	
7 5 8	15 23	20	10	8 3	4	
7 9 26	16 24	21	10	48 3	5	
7 13 44	17 25	22	11	28 4	6	
7 18 1	18 26	23	12	8 5	7	
7 22 18	19 27	23	12	48 6	7	
7 26 34	20 28	24	13	28 6	8	
7 30 50	21 29	25	14	7 7	9	
7 35 5	22 29	26	14	47 8	10	
7 39 20	23 ♍	26	15	27 9	11	
7 43 34	24 1	27	16	6 9	12	
7 47 47	25 2	28	16	45 10	13	
7 52 0	26 3	29	17	24 11	14	
7 56 12	27 4	29	18	3 12	15	
8 0 24	28 5	♎	18	42 12	16	
8 4 35	29 6	1	19	21 13	16	
8 8 45	30 6	2	19	59 14	17	

Bottom-middle

Sidereal Time (H.M.S.)	10 ♍	11 ♎	12 ♎	Ascen ♏	2 ♏	3 ♐
8 8 45	0 6	2	19	59 14	17	
8 12 54	1 7	2	20	38 15	18	
8 17 3	2 8	3	21	16 15	19	
8 21 11	3 9	4	21	55 16	20	
8 25 19	4 10	5	22	33 17	21	
8 29 26	5 11	5	23	11 18	22	
8 33 31	6 12	6	23	49 18	23	
8 37 37	7 13	7	24	26 19	24	
8 41 41	8 13	7	25	4 20	25	
8 45 45	9 14	8	25	42 20	26	
8 49 48	10 15	9	26	19 21	26	
8 53 51	11 16	10	26	56 22	27	
8 57 52	12 17	10	27	33 23	28	
9 1 53	13 18	11	28	10 23	29	
9 5 53	14 19	12	28	47 24	♐	
9 9 53	15 19	12	29	24 25	1	
9 13 52	16 20	13	0 ♐	1 25	2	
9 17 50	17 21	14	0	37 26	3	
9 21 47	18 22	15	1	13 27	4	
9 25 44	19 23	15	1	50 28	5	
9 29 40	20 24	16	2	26 28	6	
9 33 35	21 24	17	3	2 29	7	
9 37 29	22 25	17	3	38 30	7	
9 41 23	23 26	18	4	13 ♐	8	
9 45 16	24 27	19	4	49 1	9	
9 49 9	25 28	19	5	24 2	10	
9 53 1	26 29	20	6	0 3	11	
9 56 52	27 29	21	6	35 3	12	
10 0 42	28 ♎	21	7	11 4	13	
10 4 33	29 1	22	7	46 5	14	
10 8 23	30 2	23	8	21 5	15	

Bottom-right

Sidereal Time (H.M.S.)	10 ♎	11 ♎	12 ♏	Ascen ♏	2 ♐	3 ♑
10 8 23	0 2	23	8	21 5	15	
10 12 12	1 3	23	8	56 6	16	
10 16 0	2 3	24	9	31 7	17	
10 19 48	3 4	25	10	5 7	18	
10 23 35	4 5	25	10	40 8	19	
10 27 22	5 6	26	11	15 9	20	
10 31 8	6 7	27	11	49 10	21	
10 34 54	7 7	27	12	24 10	22	
10 38 40	8 8	28	12	58 11	23	
10 42 25	9 9	29	13	33 12	24	
10 46 9	10 10	29	14	7 13	25	
10 49 53	11 11	♏	14	41 14	26	
10 53 37	12 11	1	15	15 14	27	
10 57 20	13 12	1	15	50 15	28	
11 1 3	14 13	2	16	24 16	29	
11 4 46	15 14	3	16	58 16	♒	
11 8 28	16 15	3	17	32 17	1	
11 12 10	17 15	4	18	6 18	2	
11 15 52	18 16	5	18	40 19	3	
11 19 34	19 17	5	19	14 19	4	
11 23 15	20 18	6	19	48 20	5	
11 26 56	21 18	7	20	22 21	7	
11 30 37	22 19	7	20	56 21	8	
11 34 18	23 20	8	21	30 22	9	
11 37 58	24 21	8	22	4 23	10	
11 41 39	25 22	9	22	38 24	11	
11 45 20	26 22	10	23	12 25	12	
11 49 0	27 23	10	23	46 25	13	
11 52 40	28 24	11	24	21 26	15	
11 56 20	29 25	12	24	55 27	16	
12 0 0	30 26	12	25	29 28	17	

TABLES OF HOUSES FOR   Latitude 59° 56' N.

Sidereal Time	10 ♎	11 ♎	12 ♏	Ascen ♏ °	'	2 ♐	3 ♑
H. M. S.							
12 0 0	0	25	12	25	29	28	17
12 3 40	1	26	13	26	3	29	18
12 7 20	2	27	14	26	38	29	19
12 11 0	3	28	14	27	12	♑	21
12 14 41	4	28	15	27	47	1	22
12 18 21	5	29	16	28	21	2	23
12 22 2	6	♏	16	28	56	3	24
12 25 42	7	1	17	29	31	4	25
12 29 23	8	2	18	0 ♐	6	5	27
12 33 4	9	2	18	0	41	5	28
12 36 45	10	3	19	1	16	6	29
12 40 26	11	4	20	1	51	7	♓
12 44 8	12	5	20	2	27	8	2
12 47 50	13	5	21	3	2	9	3
12 51 32	14	6	22	3	38	10	5
12 55 14	15	7	22	4	14	11	6
12 58 57	16	8	23	4	50	12	7
13 2 40	17	8	23	5	27	13	9
13 6 23	18	9	24	6	3	14	10
13 10 7	19	10	25	6	40	15	11
13 13 51	20	11	25	7	17	16	13
13 17 35	21	12	26	7	54	17	14
13 21 20	22	12	27	8	32	18	15
13 25 6	23	13	27	9	9	20	17
13 28 52	24	14	28	9	47	21	18
13 32 38	25	15	29	10	26	22	20
13 36 25	26	15	29	11	4	23	21
13 40 12	27	16	♐	11	43	24	22
13 44 0	28	17	1	12	23	26	24
13 47 48	29	18	2	13	2	27	25
13 51 37	30	19	2	13	42	28	27

Sidereal Time	10 ♏	11 ♏	12 ♐	Ascen ♐ °	'	2 ♑	3 ♓
H. M. S.							
13 51 37	0	19	2	13	42	28	27
13 55 27	1	19	3	14	23	29	28
13 59 17	2	20	4	15	4	♈	
14 3 8	3	21	4	15	45	2	1
14 6 59	4	22	5	16	27	4	3
14 10 51	5	23	6	17	9	5	4
14 14 44	6	23	7	17	52	7	6
14 18 37	7	24	7	18	35	8	7
14 22 31	8	25	8	19	19	10	9
14 26 25	9	26	9	20	4	11	10
14 30 20	10	27	9	20	49	13	11
14 34 16	11	27	10	21	35	14	13
14 38 13	12	28	11	22	21	16	14
14 42 10	13	29	12	23	9	18	16
14 46 8	14	♐	12	23	57	20	17
14 50 7	15	1	13	24	46	22	19
14 54 7	16	2	14	25	36	24	20
14 58 7	17	2	15	26	27	26	22
15 2 8	18	3	16	27	18	28	23
15 6 9	19	4	16	28	11	♓	25
15 10 12	20	5	17	29	5	2	26
15 14 15	21	6	18	0 ♈	0	4	28
15 18 19	22	7	19	0	57	6	29
15 22 23	23	7	20	1	55	8	♉
15 26 29	24	8	21	2	54	11	2
15 30 35	25	9	21	3	55	13	3
15 34 41	26	10	22	4	58	15	5
15 38 49	27	11	23	6	2	18	6
15 42 57	28	12	24	7	8	20	7
15 47 6	29	13	25	8	17	22	9
15 51 15	30	14	26	9	28	25	10

Sidereal Time	10 ♐	11 ♐	12 ♐	Ascen ♑ °	'	2 ♓	3 ♉
H. M. S.							
15 51 15	0	14	26	9	28	25	10
15 55 25	1	14	27	10	41	27	12
15 59 36	2	15	28	11	56	♈	13
16 3 48	3	16	29	13	15	2	14
16 8 0	4	17	♑	14	36	5	16
16 12 13	5	18	1	16	1	7	17
16 16 26	6	19	2	17	30	10	18
16 20 40	7	20	3	19	2	12	20
16 24 55	8	21	4	20	39	15	21
16 29 10	9	22	5	22	20	17	22
16 33 26	10	23	6	24	7	19	23
16 37 42	11	24	7	25	58	22	25
16 41 59	12	25	8	27	56	24	26
16 46 16	13	26	9	0 ♒	1	26	27
16 50 34	14	27	10	2	13	29	28
16 54 52	15	28	11	5	18	1	♊
16 59 10	16	29	12	7	0	3	1
17 3 29	17	♑	13	9	37	5	2
17 7 49	18	1	15	12	23	7	3
17 12 9	19	2	16	15	21	9	5
17 16 29	20	3	17	18	29	11	6
17 20 49	21	4	18	21	49	13	7
17 25 9	22	5	20	25	21	15	8
17 29 30	23	6	21	29	6	17	9
17 33 51	24	7	22	3 ♓	22	19	10
17 38 12	25	8	24	7	10	21	11
17 42 34	26	9	25	11	23	23	12
17 46 55	27	10	27	15	58	24	14
17 51 17	28	11	28	20	16	26	15
17 55 38	29	12	♒	25	16	27	16
18 0 0	30	13	1	30	1	0	29 17

Sidereal Time	10 ♑	11 ♑	12 ♒	Ascen ♈ °	'	2 ♉	3 ♊
H. M. S.							
18 0 0	0	13	1	0	0	29	17
18 4 22	1	14	3	4	44	♉	18
18 8 43	2	15	4	9	26	2	19
18 13 5	3	16	6	14	2	3	20
18 17 26	4	17	8	18	30	5	21
18 21 48	5	19	9	22	50	6	22
18 26 9	6	20	11	26	58	6	22
18 30 30	7	21	13	0 ♊54		9	24
18 34 51	8	22	15	4	39	10	25
18 39 11	9	23	17	8	11	12	26
18 43 31	10	24	19	11	31	13	27
18 47 51	11	25	21	14	39	14	28
18 52 11	12	27	23	17	37	15	29
18 56 31	13	28	25	20	23	17	♋
19 0 50	14	29	27	23	0	18	1
19 5 8	15	♒	29	25	28	19	2
19 9 26	16	2	♓	27	48	20	3
19 13 44	17	3	4	29	59	21	4
19 18 1	18	4	6	2 ♊	4	22	5
19 22 18	19	5	8	4	2	23	5
19 26 34	20	7	11	5	53	24	7
19 30 50	21	8	13	7	40	25	8
19 35 5	22	9	15	9	21	26	8
19 39 20	23	10	18	10	58	28	10
19 43 34	24	12	20	12	30	29	11
19 47 47	25	13	23	13	59	♋	12
19 52 0	26	14	25	15	24	1	13
19 56 12	27	16	28	16	45	2	14
20 0 24	28	17	♈	18	4	2	15
20 4 35	29	18	3	19	3	3	16
20 8 45	30	20	5	20	32	4	16

Sidereal Time	10 ♒	11 ♒	12 ♈	Ascen ♊ °	'	2 ♋	3 ♋
H. M. S.							
20 8 45	0	20	5	20	32	4	16
20 12 54	1	21	8	21	43	5	17
20 17 3	2	23	10	22	52	6	18
20 21 11	3	24	12	23	58	7	19
20 25 19	4	25	15	25	2	8	20
20 29 26	5	27	17	26	5	9	21
20 33 31	6	28	19	27	6	9	22
20 37 37	7	♈	22	28	5	10	23
20 41 41	8	1	24	29	1	11	23
20 45 45	9	2	26	0 ♋	12	12	24
20 49 48	10	4	28	0	55	13	25
20 53 51	11	5	♉	1	49	14	26
20 57 52	12	7	2	2	42	14	27
21 1 53	13	8	4	3	33	15	28
21 5 53	14	10	6	4	24	16	28
21 9 53	15	11	8	5	14	17	29
21 13 52	16	13	10	6	3	18	♌
21 17 50	17	14	12	6	51	18	1
21 21 47	18	16	14	7	39	19	2
21 25 44	19	17	15	8	25	20	2
21 29 40	20	19	17	9	11	21	3
21 33 35	21	20	19	9	56	21	4
21 37 29	22	21	20	10	41	22	5
21 41 23	23	23	22	11	25	23	6
21 45 16	24	24	23	12	7	23	7
21 49 9	25	26	25	12	51	24	7
21 53 1	26	27	26	13	33	25	8
21 56 52	27	29	28	14	15	26	9
22 0 43	28	♉	29	14	56	26	10
22 4 33	29	2	♊	15	37	27	11
22 8 23	30	3	2	16	18	28	11

Sidereal Time	10 ♓	11 ♈	12 ♊	Ascen ♋ °	'	2 ♌	3 ♌
H. M. S.							
22 8 23	0	3	2	16	18	28	11
22 12 12	1	5	3	16	58	29	12
22 16 0	2	6	4	17	37	29	13
22 19 48	3	8	6	18	17	♌	14
22 23 35	4	9	7	18	56	1	15
22 27 22	5	10	8	19	34	1	15
22 31 8	6	12	9	20	13	2	16
22 34 54	7	13	10	20	51	3	17
22 38 40	8	15	11	21	28	3	18
22 42 25	9	16	12	22	6	4	18
22 46 9	10	17	14	22	43	5	19
22 49 53	11	19	15	23	20	5	20
22 53 37	12	20	16	24	57	6	21
22 57 20	13	21	17	24	33	7	22
23 1 3	14	23	18	25	10	7	22
23 4 46	15	24	19	26	46	8	23
23 8 28	16	26	20	26	20	9	24
23 12 10	17	27	21	27	58	9	24
23 15 52	18	28	22	27	33	10	25
23 19 34	19	♊	23	28	9	11	26
23 23 15	20	♋	24	28	44	11	27
23 26 56	21	2	25	29	19	12	28
23 30 37	22	3	25	29	54	12	28
23 34 18	23	5	26	0 ♌	29	13	29
23 37 58	24	6	27	1	3	14	♍
23 41 39	25	7	28	1	39	14	1
23 45 19	26	8	29	2	13	15	2
23 49 0	27	9	♋	2	48	16	2
23 52 40	28	11	1	3	22	16	3
23 56 20	29	12	2	3	57	17	4
24 0 0	30	13	2	4	31	18	5

Reprinted with the kind permission of ARIES PRESS.

TABLES OF HOUSES FOR THE — Latitude 59° 0' N.

Sidereal Time H. M. S.	10 ♈	11 ♉	12 ♋	Ascen ♌ (° ')	2 ♌	3 ♍
0 0 0	0	12	9	3 31	17	4
0 3 40	1	13	10	4 6	17	5
0 7 20	2	14	11	4 41	18	6
0 11 1	3	15	11	5 16	19	7
0 14 41	4	17	12	5 51	19	7
0 18 21	5	18	13	6 26	20	8
0 22 2	6	19	13	7 1	21	9
0 25 42	7	20	14	7 35	21	10
0 29 23	8	21	15	8 10	22	10
0 33 4	9	22	15	8 45	23	11
0 36 45	10	23	16	9 20	23	12
0 40 27	11	24	17	9 54	24	13
0 44 8	12	26	17	10 29	25	14
0 47 50	13	27	18	11 4	25	14
0 51 32	14	28	18	11 39	26	15
0 55 14	15	29	19	12 13	27	16
0 58 57	16	♊	19	12 48	27	17
1 2 40	17	1	20	13 23	28	18
1 6 24	18	2	20	13 58	29	18
1 10 7	19	3	21	14 33	29	19
1 13 51	20	4	21	15 8	♍	20
1 17 36	21	5	22	15 43	1	21
1 21 21	22	6	22	16 18	1	22
1 25 6	23	7	23	16 53	2	22
1 28 52	24	8	23	17 28	3	23
1 32 38	25	9	19	18 3	3	24
1 36 25	26	10	20	18 39	4	25
1 40 13	27	11	21	19 14	5	26
1 44 1	28	12	22	19 49	5	27
1 47 49	29	13	22	20 25	6	27
1 51 38	30	14	23	21 1	7	28

Sidereal Time H. M. S.	10 ♉	11 ♊	12 ♋	Ascen ♌ (° ')	2 ♍	3 ♍
1 51 38	0	14	23	21 1	7	28
1 55 28	1	15	24	21 36	7	29
1 59 18	2	16	25	22 12	8	♍
2 3 8	3	17	25	22 48	9	1
2 7 0	4	18	26	23 24	9	2
2 10 52	5	19	27	24 0	10	2
2 14 44	6	19	27	24 36	11	3
2 18 37	7	20	28	25 13	12	4
2 22 31	8	21	29	25 49	12	5
2 26 26	9	22	30	26 26	13	6
2 30 21	10	23	♌	27 2	14	7
2 34 17	11	24	1	27 39	14	7
2 38 14	12	25	2	28 16	15	8
2 42 11	13	26	3	28 53	16	9
2 46 9	14	27	3	29 30	16	10
2 50	15	28	4	0 ♍ 7	17	11
2 54	16	29	5	0 45	18	12
2 58	17	♋	5	1 22	19	13
3 2	18	1	6	2 0	19	13
3 6	19	2	7	2 37	20	14
3 10	20	3	8	3 15	21	15
3 14	21	3	8	3 53	22	16
3 18	22	4	9	4 31	22	17
3 22	23	5	10	5 10	23	18
3 26	24	6	11	5 48	24	19
3 30 35	25	7	11	6 27	25	10
3 34 42	26	8	12	7 5	25	20
3 38 49	27	9	13	7 44	26	21
3 42 57	28	10	14	8 23	27	22
3 47 6	29	11	14	9 2	28	23
3 51 16	30	12	15	9 41	28	24

Sidereal Time H. M. S.	10 ♊	11 ♋	12 ♌	Ascen ♍ (° ')	2 ♍	3 ♎
3 51 16	0	12	15	9 41	28	24
3 55 26	1	12	16	10 20	29	25
3 59 37	2	13	17	11 0	♎	26
4 3 48	3	14	17	11 39	1	27
4 8 1	4	15	18	12 19	1	28
4 12 13	5	16	19	12 59	2	28
4 16 27	6	17	20	13 39	3	29
4 20 41	7	18	20	14 19	4	♏
4 24 55	8	19	21	14 59	5	1
4 29 11	9	20	22	15 39	5	2
4 33 26	10	21	23	16 19	6	3
4 37 42	11	22	24	17 0	7	4
4 41 59	12	22	24	17 40	8	5
4 46 17	13	23	25	18 21	9	6
4 50 34	14	24	26	19 1	9	7
4 54 52	15	25	27	19 42	10	7
4 59 11	16	26	27	20 23	11	8
5 3 30	17	27	28	21 4	12	9
5 7 49	18	28	29	21 45	13	10
5 12 9	19	29	30	22 26	13	11
5 16 29	20	♌	♍ 23	7 14	12	—
5 20 49	21	1	1	23 48	15	13
5 25 10	22	2	2	24 29	16	14
5 29 30	23	3	3	25 10	17	15
5 33 51	24	3	4	25 52	17	16
5 38 13	25	4	4	26 33	18	16
5 42 34	26	5	5	27 14	19	17
5 46 55	27	6	6	27 56	20	18
5 51 17	28	7	7	28 37	20	19
5 55 38	29	8	7	29 19	21	20
6 0 0	30	9	8	30 0	22	21

Sidereal Time H. M. S.	10 ♋	11 ♌	12 ♍	Ascen ♎ (° ')	2 ♎	3 ♏
6 0 0	0	9	8	0 22	21	—
6 4 22	1	10	9	0 41	23	22
6 8 43	2	11	10	1 23	23	23
6 13 5	3	12	11	2 4	24	24
6 17 26	4	13	11	2 46	25	25
6 21 47	5	13	12	3 27	26	26
6 26 9	6	14	13	4 8	27	27
6 30 30	7	15	14	4 50	28	28
6 34 50	8	16	15	5 31	28	28
6 39 11	9	17	15	6 12	29	29
6 43 31	10	18	16	6 53	♏	1
6 47 51	11	19	17	7 34	1	1
6 52 11	12	20	18	8 15	2	2
6 56 30	13	21	18	8 56	2	3
7 0 49	14	22	19	9 37	3	4
7 5 8	15	23	20	10 18	4	5
7 9 26	16	24	21	10 59	5	6
7 13 43	17	24	22	11 39	5	7
7 18 1	18	25	22	12 20	6	8
7 22 18	19	26	23	13 0	7	8
7 26 34	20	27	24	13 41	7	9
7 30 49	21	28	24	14 21	8	10
7 35 5	22	29	25	15 1	9	11
7 39 19	23	♍	26	15 41	10	12
7 43 33	24	1	27	16 21	10	13
7 47 47	25	2	28	17 1	11	14
7 51 59	26	2	29	17 41	12	15
7 56 12	27	3	29	18 21	13	16
8 0 23	28	4	♎	19 0	13	17
8 4 34	29	5	1	19 40	14	18
8 8 44	30	6	2	20 19	15	18

Sidereal Time H. M. S.	10 ♌	11 ♍	12 ♎	Ascen ♎ (° ')	2 ♏	3 ♐
8 8 44	0	6	2	20 19	15	18
8 12 54	1	7	2	20 58	16	19
8 17 3	2	8	3	21 37	17	20
8 21 11	3	9	4	22 16	18	21
8 25 19	4	10	5	22 55	18	22
8 29 25	5	10	5	23 33	19	23
8 33 31	6	11	6	24 12	20	24
8 37 36	7	12	7	24 50	21	25
8 41 41	8	13	8	25 29	21	26
8 45 44	9	14	8	26 7	22	27
8 49 48	10	15	9	26 45	23	28
8 53 50	11	16	10	27 23	23	28
8 57 52	12	17	11	28 0	24	29
9 1 52	13	17	11	28 38	25	♑
9 5 53	14	18	12	29 15	25	1
9 9 51	15	19	13	29 53	26	2
9 13 51	16	20	14	0 ♏ 30	27	3
9 17 49	17	21	14	1 7	27	4
9 21 46	18	22	15	1 44	28	5
9 25 43	19	23	16	2 21	29	6
9 29 39	20	23	16	2 58	30	7
9 33 34	21	24	17	3 34	♐	8
9 37 29	22	25	18	4 11	1	9
9 41 23	23	26	19	4 47	2	10
9 45 16	24	27	19	5 24	3	11
9 49 8	25	28	20	6 0	3	12
9 53 0	26	28	21	6 36	4	12
9 56 52	27	29	22	7 12	5	13
10 0 42	28	♎	22	7 48	5	14
10 4 32	29	1	23	8 24	6	15
10 8 22	30	2	24	8 59	7	16

Sidereal Time H. M. S.	10 ♍	11 ♎	12 ♏	Ascen ♏ (° ')	2 ♐	3 ♑
10 8 22	0	2	24	8 59	7	16
10 12 11	1	3	24	9 35	8	17
10 15 59	2	3	25	10 11	8	18
10 19 47	3	4	26	10 46	9	19
10 23 35	4	5	26	11 21	10	20
10 27 22	5	6	27	11 57	11	21
10 31 8	6	7	28	12 32	11	22
10 34 54	7	8	28	13 7	12	23
10 38 39	8	9	29	13 42	13	24
10 42 24	9	9	29	14 17	14	25
10 46 9	10	10	♏	14 52	14	26
10 49 53	11	11	1	15 27	15	27
10 53 36	12	12	2	16 2	16	28
10 57 20	13	12	2	16 37	17	29
11 1 3	14	13	3	17 12	17	♒
11 4 46	15	14	3	17 47	18	1
11 8 28	16	15	4	18 21	19	2
11 12 10	17	16	5	18 56	20	3
11 15 52	18	17	5	19 31	20	4
11 19 33	19	17	6	20 6	21	6
11 23 15	20	18	7	20 42	22	7
11 26 56	21	19	7	21 15	23	8
11 30 37	22	20	8	21 50	24	9
11 34 18	23	20	9	22 25	24	10
11 37 58	24	21	9	22 59	25	11
11 41 39	25	22	10	23 34	26	12
11 45 19	26	23	11	24 9	27	13
11 48 59	27	24	11	24 44	27	14
11 52 40	28	24	12	25 19	28	16
11 56 20	29	25	13	25 54	29	17
12 0 0	30	26	13	26 29	30	18

Reprinted with the kind permission of ARIES PRESS.

TABLES OF HOUSES FOR THE   Latitude 59° 0' N.

Sidereal Time H. M. S.	10 ♎	11 ♎	12 ♏	Ascen ♏ ° '	2 ♑	3 ♒
12 0 0	0	26	13	26 29	0	18
12 3 40	1	27	14	27 4	1	19
12 7 20	2	27	15	27 39	2	20
12 11 1	3	28	16	28 15	3	21
12 14 41	4	29	16	28 50	3	23
12 18 21	5	♏0	17	29 25	4	24
12 22 2	6	1	17	0♐1	5	25
12 25 42	7	1	18	0 37	6	26
12 29 23	8	2	19	1 13	7	28
12 33 4	9	3	20	1 49	8	29
12 36 45	10	4	20	2 25	9	♓0
12 40 27	11	4	21	3 1	10	1
12 44 8	12	5	22	3 37	11	3
12 47 50	13	6	22	4 14	12	4
12 51 32	14	7	23	4 51	13	5
12 55 14	15	8	24	5 28	14	6
12 58 57	16	8	24	6 5	15	8
13 2 40	17	9	25	6 42	16	9
13 6 24	18	10	26	7 20	17	10
13 10 7	19	11	26	7 58	18	12
13 13 51	20	12	27	8 36	19	13
13 17 36	21	12	28	9 14	20	14
13 21 21	22	13	29	9 53	21	16
13 25 6	23	14	29	10 32	22	17
13 28 52	24	15	♐0	11 11	23	19
13 32 38	25	16	1	11 51	25	20
13 36 25	26	16	1	12 31	26	21
13 40 13	27	17	2	13 11	27	23
13 44 1	28	18	3	13 52	28	24
13 47 49	29	19	3	14 33	♒0	25
13 51 38	30	19	4	15 14	1	27

Sidereal Time H. M. S.	10 ♏	11 ♏	12 ♐	Ascen ♐ ° '	2 ♒	3 ♓
13 51 38	0	19	4	15 14	1	27
13 55 28	1	20	5	15 56	2	28
13 59 18	2	21	6	16 38	4	♈0
14 3 8	3	22	6	17 21	5	1
14 7 0	4	23	7	18 4	6	3
14 10 52	5	24	7	18 48	8	4
14 14 44	6	24	8	19 33	9	5
14 18 37	7	25	9	20 18	11	7
14 22 31	8	26	10	21 4	12	8
14 26 26	9	27	11	21 50	14	10
14 30 21	10	28	12	22 37	16	11
14 34 17	11	29	13	23 25	17	12
14 38 14	12	29	13	24 13	19	14
14 42 11	13	♐0	14	25 2	21	15
14 46 9	14	1	14	25 53	22	17
14 50 9	15	2	15	26 44	24	18
14 54 7	16	3	16	27 36	26	19
14 58 8	17	4	17	28 29	28	21
15 2 8	18	4	18	29 23	♓0	22
15 6 10	19	5	18	0♑18	2	24
15 10 12	20	6	19	1 16	4	25
15 14 16	21	7	20	2 9	6	26
15 18 19	22	8	21	3 11	8	28
15 22 24	23	9	22	4 12	10	29
15 26 29	24	10	23	5 14	12	♉0
15 30 35	25	11	23	6 18	14	2
15 34 42	26	11	24	7 23	16	3
15 38 49	27	12	25	8 31	18	5
15 42 57	28	13	26	9 40	21	6
15 47 6	29	14	27	10 52	23	7
15 51 16	30	15	28	12 6	25	9

Sidereal Time H. M. S.	10 ♐	11 ♐	12 ♐	Ascen ♑ ° '	2 ♓	3 ♉
15 51 16	0	15	28	12 6	25	9
15 55 26	1	16	29	13 22	28	11
15 59 37	2	16	♑0	14 41	♈0	12
16 3 48	3	17	1	16 3	2	13
16 8 1	4	18	2	17 28	4	15
16 12 13	5	19	3	18 56	6	16
16 16 27	6	20	4	20 28	9	17
16 20 41	7	21	5	22 5	11	19
16 24 55	8	22	6	23 45	14	20
16 29 11	9	23	7	25 29	16	21
16 33 26	10	24	8	27 19	18	22
16 37 42	11	25	9	29 14	20	24
16 41 59	12	26	10	1♒14	22	25
16 46 17	13	27	11	3 21	25	26
16 50 34	14	28	12	5 34	27	27
16 54 52	15	29	14	7 54	29	29
16 59 11	16	♑0	15	10 22	♉0	♊0
17 3 30	17	1	16	12 58	3	1
17 7 49	18	2	17	15 43	5	2
17 12 9	19	3	18	18 36	7	3
17 16 29	20	4	20	21 39	9	4
17 20 40	21	5	21	24 52	11	6
17 25 10	22	6	22	28 14	12	7
17 29 30	23	7	24	1♓46	14	8
17 33 51	24	8	25	5 27	16	9
17 38 13	25	9	26	9 17	18	10
17 42 34	26	10	28	13 15	20	11
17 46 55	27	11	29	17 21	21	12
17 51 17	28	12	♒0	21 30	22	14
17 55 38	29	13	2	25 44	25	15
18 0 0	30	14	4	30 0	26	16

Sidereal Time H. M. S.	10 ♑	11 ♑	12 ♒	Ascen ♈ ° '	2 ♉	3 ♊
18 0 0	0	14	4	0 0	26	16
18 4 22	1	15	6	4 16	28	17
18 8 43	2	16	7	8 30	♉0	18
18 13 5	3	17	9	12 40	1	19
18 17 26	4	19	10	16 45	2	20
18 21 47	5	20	12	20 43	4	21
18 26 9	6	21	14	24 33	5	22
18 30 30	7	22	16	28 14	6	23
18 34 50	8	23	18	1♉46	8	24
18 39 11	9	24	19	5 8	9	25
18 43 31	10	26	21	8 21	10	26
18 47 51	11	27	23	11 24	12	27
18 52 11	12	28	25	14 17	13	28
18 56 30	13	29	27	17 2	14	29
19 0 49	14	♒0	29	19 38	15	♋0
19 5 8	15	1	♓2	22 6	16	1
19 9 26	16	3	3	24 26	18	2
19 13 43	17	4	5	26 39	19	3
19 18 1	18	5	8	28 46	20	4
19 22 18	19	6	10	0♊11	21	5
19 26 34	20	8	12	2 41	22	6
19 30 49	21	9	14	4 31	23	7
19 35 5	22	10	17	6 15	24	8
19 39 19	23	12	19	7 55	25	9
19 43 33	24	13	21	9 32	26	10
19 47 47	25	14	23	11 4	27	11
19 51 59	26	16	26	12 32	28	12
19 56 12	27	17	28	13 57	29	13
20 0 23	28	18	♈0	15 19	♋0	14
20 4 34	29	19	2	16 38	1	14
20 8 44	30	21	5	17 54	2	15

Sidereal Time H. M. S.	10 ♒	11 ♒	12 ♈	Ascen ♊ ° '	2 ♋	3 ♋
20 8 44	0	21	5	17 54	2	15
20 12 54	1	22	7	19 8	3	16
20 17 3	2	23	9	20 20	4	17
20 21 11	3	25	11	21 29	5	18
20 25 18	4	26	14	22 37	6	19
20 29 25	5	28	16	23 46	7	20
20 33 31	6	29	18	24 46	7	21
20 37 36	7	♈0	20	25 48	8	22
20 41 41	8	2	22	26 49	9	22
20 45 44	9	3	24	27 48	10	23
20 49 48	10	5	26	28 45	11	24
20 53 50	11	6	28	29 42	12	25
20 57 52	12	7	♉0	0♋37	12	26
21 1 52	13	9	2	1 31	13	27
21 5 53	14	10	4	2 24	14	28
21 9 51	15	12	6	3 16	15	28
21 13 51	16	13	8	4 7	16	29
21 17 49	17	15	9	4 58	16	♌0
21 21 46	18	16	11	5 47	17	1
21 25 43	19	17	13	6 35	18	2
21 29 39	20	19	14	7 23	19	3
21 33 34	21	20	16	8 10	20	3
21 37 29	22	22	18	8 56	20	4
21 41 23	23	23	19	9 42	21	5
21 45 16	24	25	21	10 27	22	6
21 49 8	25	26	22	11 12	23	7
21 53 0	26	27	24	11 56	23	7
21 56 52	27	29	25	12 39	24	8
22 0 42	28	♉0	26	13 22	25	8
22 4 32	29	2	28	14 4	26	10
22 8 22	30	3	29	14 46	26	11

Sidereal Time H. M. S.	10 ♓	11 ♈	12 ♉	Ascen ♋ ° '	2 ♋	3 ♌
22 8 22	0	3	29	14 46	26	11
22 12 11	1	4	♊0	15 27	27	11
22 15 59	2	6	2	16 8	28	12
22 19 47	3	7	3	16 49	28	13
22 23 35	4	9	4	17 29	29	14
22 27 22	5	10	6	18 9	♌0	15
22 31 8	6	11	7	18 48	1	15
22 34 54	7	13	8	19 28	1	16
22 38 39	8	14	9	20 7	1	17
22 42 24	9	16	10	20 46	2	18
22 46 9	10	17	11	21 24	3	19
22 49 53	11	18	12	22 2	4	19
22 53 36	12	20	13	22 40	5	20
22 57 20	13	21	14	23 18	5	21
23 1 1	14	22	15	23 55	6	22
23 4 46	15	23	16	24 32	7	22
23 8 28	16	24	17	25 9	7	23
23 12 10	17	26	18	25 46	8	24
23 15 52	18	27	19	26 23	9	25
23 19 33	19	29	20	26 59	9	26
23 23 13	20	♉0	21	27 35	10	26
23 26 56	21	1	22	28 11	11	27
23 30 37	22	2	23	28 47	11	28
23 34 18	23	3	24	29 23	12	29
23 37 58	24	4	25	29 59	13	29
23 41 39	25	6	26	0♌35	13	♍0
23 45 19	26	7	27	1 10	14	1
23 48 59	27	9	28	1 45	15	2
23 52 40	28	10	28	2 21	15	3
23 56 20	29	11	29	2 56	16	3
24 0 0	30	12	30	3 31	17	4

APPENDIX F
DEGREES OR HOURS INTO DECIMALS

M.	Dec.	M.	Dec.
1	.02	16	.27
2	.03	17	.28
3	.05	18	.30
4	.07	19	.32
5	.08	20	.33
6	.10	21	.35
7	.12	22	.37
8	.13	23	.38
9	.15	24	.40
10	.17	25	.42
11	.18	26	.43
12	.20	27	.45
13	.22	28	.47
14	.23	29	.48
15	.25	30	.50

MINUTES EXPRESSED AS DECIMALS OF A DEGREE

M.	Dec.	M.	Dec.
31	.52	46	.77
32	.53	47	.78
33	.55	48	.80
34	.57	49	.82
35	.58	50	.83
36	.60	51	.85
37	.62	52	.87
38	.63	53	.88
39	.65	54	.90
40	.67	55	.92
41	.68	56	.93
42	.70	57	.95
43	.72	58	.97
44	.73	59	.98
45	.75	60	1.00

APPENDIX G
THE SLIDE RULE

Since the slide rule lends itself so ably in calculating proportion—the basis for all astrological computations—its use will be briefly described here.

The slide rule consists of three basic parts: the *body* or frame; the *slide*, the movable rule that slides back and forth in the middle of the body; and the *cursor*, a hairline inscribed on a transparent piece that moves over the top of the body and slide.

Most rules have a variety of scales imprinted on both the front and back (usually) of the body and slide; the hairline assists in the reading. Various rules have a number of different scales, but all have the *C scale* and the *D scale*. These two scales are used in proportion.

The C scale is on the lower edge of the slide, and directly adjacent to it is the D scale on the body. Both are clearly labeled.

It should be noted that with the rule in the closed position, the C and D scales are identical. The numbers running the length of the rule, 1 through 10 (the 10 expressed as 1) are the *primary* numbers. As the numbers are in a logarithmic sequence, they are not evenly spaced.

The major divisions between the primary numbers are the *secondary* numbers. Usually the secondary numbers between 1 and 2 are the only ones actually numbered on the rule. If the hairline were set over the secondary number 5 between primary 1 and 2, the indicated number would then be 15 (or 1.5 or 150, etc., depending upon the placement of the decimal point).

The next division is the *tertiary*. Tertiary numbers are between secondary numbers. Between primary 1 and 2, the tertiary divisions are marked off in tenths; between primary 2 and 4, the tertiary divisions are in fifths (two-tenths); and on the balance of the rule they are in halves.

With the hairline set at the third division from the secondary 8 between primary 1 and 2, the number is 183 (primary 1, secondary 8, tertiary 3). If the hairline is set at the division between secondary 3 and 4 following primary 4, the number is 435.

If in the last number, 435, the hairline were set slightly to the right of the tertiary 5 division, the number would actually be 436 (or perhaps 437). Whenever the hairline is not directly on a division inscribed on the rule, the tertiary number must then be estimated. Some practice is necessary to become adept in reading a slide rule. Generally a rule is not intended to provide much accuracy beyond three significant figures.

The use of the rule in proportion is best explained by actual example. Take the rule and move the slide so that 2 on the C scale appears over 4 on the D scale. This indicates a fraction, 2 over 4. Note that the 1 on the C scale is over the 2 on the D scale, indicating 1 over 2, or ½. At this placement, then, the entire rule is set up so that there are an infinite number of fractions all equal to ½: There is 1.5 on the C scale over 3 on the D scale (½), 2.1 over 4.2 (½), 4.5 over 9, 5 over 10, and so on.

Part of the C scale is extended beyond the body, however. To read the same proportional fraction (½) for these numbers, move the slide so that the right-hand 1 on the C scale (either 1 on the C scale is called an *index*) is over 2 on the D scale. Now 6 appears over 12, 9.5 over 19, etc.

A typical proportion might be:

$$\frac{3}{4} = \frac{?}{8}$$

To solve simply set up the fraction, 3 over 4 (3 on the C scale over 4 on the D scale), locate 8 on the D scale with the hairline and read 6, the answer.

Another proportion:

$$\frac{25}{65} = \frac{?}{190}$$

Since this involves numbers that are not as readily apparent to the eye as those before, make use of the hairline. First set the hairline to 65 on the D scale, then move the slide so that 25 on the C scale appears directly under the hairline. Now the left number of the proportion, 25 over 65, is set. It becomes immediately apparent that there is only empty space over 190 on the D scale, so the indices must first be shifted.

Move the hairline over the left index (the 1) on the C scale, then move the slide so that the right index appears under the hairline. Now move the hairline over to 190; the answer is 73.

The ordinary rule does not read degrees and minutes; the minutes must first be changed to a decimal of a degree. Appendix F supplies this information. A good example of the use of a slide rule in astrological computation may be had by referring to Figure 48 in the text, the Stockholm Planets Work Sheet.

The basic proportion is:

$$\frac{4hr\ 4min}{24hr} = \frac{c}{d}$$

The daily motion is d, the unknown portion of this is c. First it is necessary to change 4hr 4 min to a decimal. This becomes 4.07 hours.

Locate 24 on the D scale with the hairline. Over it place 4.07. (4.07 must be estimated; the space between primary 4 and the first secondary division, 4.1, must be mentally divided into tenths. The division 7 would then fall somewhat to the right of the inscribed tertiary 5 position—the 7 in 4.07 is a tertiary division.)

With this position "locked in," it is merely a matter of locating the various daily motion values on the D scale and reading the proportion c on the C scale. (The letter similarity is a coincidence.) For the Sun, d is 58'; using the hairline to locate this on the D scale the C scale provides the answer, 9.85. Since the answer need be only to the nearest minute, it is rounded off to 10. (Actually, the experienced user would never go to the trouble of reading the decimal; he simply would note the fact that the reading was greater than 9.5 and immediately round it to 10.)

The Moon's daily motion is $12° 15'$; changed to a decimal, this becomes 12.25 degrees. Opposite 12.25 on the D scale is 2.08 on the C scale; 2.08 degrees is $2° 5'$, the same as on the work sheet.

For Venus, the $1° 12'$ is better changed to 72 minutes rather than a decimal. To find this value on the C scale, it is first necessary to shift indices. Then, opposite 72 the answer is 12. (Actually 12 point something; the "something" being obviously less than .5 is dropped without further ado.)

For the house, the procedure is exactly the same. For Stockholm, Figure 49, the proportion is 20 minutes over 56 minutes equals c over d. The eleventh house in the top row shows a "diff." of $1°$. Change this to 60', locate 60 on the D scale and the answer, rounded off, is 21.

The twelfth house shows a "diff." of $2°$. Change this to 120', shift indices, and find the answer 43. And so on.

Complete directions come with any purchased slide rule; these, necessarily brief, are meant only to supplement. For the newcomer to the slide rule, it is advisable to first work the problem using logs, then use the rule to check the answer.

TABLE OF PROPORTIONAL LOGARITHMS

Hours or Degrees

Min.	0	1	2	3	4	5	6	7	8	9	10	11	Min.
0	3.1584	1.3802	1.0792	9031	7781	6812	6021	5351	4771	4260	3802	3388	0
1	3.1584	1.3730	1.0756	9007	7763	6798	6009	5341	4762	4252	3795	3382	1
2	2.8573	1.3660	1.0720	8983	7745	6784	5997	5330	4753	4244	3788	3375	2
3	2.6812	1.3590	1.0685	8959	7728	6769	5985	5320	4744	4236	3780	3368	3
4	2.5563	1.3522	1.0649	8935	7710	6755	5973	5310	4735	4228	3773	3362	4
5	2.4594	1.3454	1.0614	8912	7692	6741	5961	5300	4726	4220	3766	3355	5
6	2.3802	1.3388	1.0580	8888	7674	6726	5949	5289	4717	4212	3759	3349	6
7	2.3133	1.3323	1.0546	8865	7657	6712	5937	5279	4708	4204	3752	3342	7
8	2.2553	1.3258	1.0511	8842	7639	6698	5925	5269	4699	4196	3745	3336	8
9	2.2041	1.3195	1.0478	8819	7622	6684	5913	5259	4690	4188	3738	3329	9
10	2.1584	1.3133	1.0444	8796	7604	6670	5902	5249	4682	4180	3730	3323	10
11	2.1170	1.3071	1.0411	8773	7587	6656	5890	5239	4673	4172	3723	3316	11
12	2.0792	1.3010	1.0378	8751	7570	6642	5878	5229	4664	4164	3716	3310	12
13	2.0444	1.2950	1.0345	8728	7552	6628	5866	5219	4655	4156	3709	3303	13
14	2.0122	1.2891	1.0313	8706	7535	6614	5855	5209	4646	4149	3702	3297	14
15	1.9823	1.2833	1.0280	8683	7518	6600	5843	5199	4638	4141	3695	3291	15
16	1.9542	1.2775	1.0248	8661	7501	6587	5832	5189	4629	4133	3688	3284	16
17	1.9279	1.2719	1.0216	8639	7484	6573	5820	5179	4620	4125	3681	3278	17
18	1.9031	1.2663	1.0185	8617	7467	6559	5809	5169	4611	4117	3674	3271	18
19	1.8796	1.2607	1.0153	8595	7451	6546	5797	5159	4603	4109	3667	3265	19
20	1.8573	1.2553	1.0122	8573	7434	6532	5786	5149	4594	4102	3660	3258	20
21	1.8361	1.2499	1.0091	8552	7417	6519	5774	5139	4585	4094	3653	3252	21
22	1.8159	1.2445	1.0061	8530	7401	6505	5763	5129	4577	4086	3646	3246	22
23	1.7966	1.2393	1.0030	8509	7384	6492	5752	5120	4568	4079	3639	3239	23
24	1.7781	1.2341	1.0000	8487	7368	6478	5740	5110	4559	4071	3632	3233	24
25	1.7604	1.2289	0.9970	8466	7351	6465	5729	5100	4551	4063	3625	3227	25
26	1.7434	1.2239	0.9940	8445	7335	6451	5718	5090	4542	4055	3618	3220	26
27	1.7270	1.2188	0.9910	8424	7318	6438	5706	5081	4534	4048	3611	3214	27
28	1.7112	1.2139	0.9881	8403	7302	6425	5692	5071	4525	4040	3604	3208	28
29	1.6969	1.2090	0.9852	8382	7286	6412	5684	5061	4516	4032	3597	3201	29
30	1.6812	1.2041	0.9823	8361	7270	6398	5673	5051	4508	4025	3590	3195	30
31	1.6670	1.1993	0.9794	8341	7254	6385	5662	5042	4499	4017	3583	3189	31
32	1.6532	1.1946	0.9765	8321	7238	6372	5651	5032	4491	4010	3577	3183	32
33	1.6398	1.1899	0.9737	8300	7222	6359	5640	5023	4482	4002	3570	3176	33
34	1.6269	1.1852	0.9708	8279	7206	6346	5629	5013	4474	3995	3563	3170	34
35	1.6143	1.1806	0.9680	8259	7190	6333	5618	5003	4466	3987	3556	3164	35
36	1.6021	1.1761	0.9652	8239	7174	6320	5607	4994	4457	3979	3549	3157	36
37	1.5902	1.1716	0.9625	8219	7159	6307	5596	4984	4449	3972	3542	3151	37
38	1.5786	1.1671	0.9597	8199	7143	6294	5585	4975	4440	3964	3535	3145	38
39	1.5673	1.1627	0.9570	8179	7128	6282	5574	4965	4432	3957	3529	3139	39
40	1.5563	1.1584	0.9542	8159	7112	6269	5563	4956	4424	3949	3522	3133	40
41	1.5456	1.1540	0.9515	8140	7097	6256	5552	4947	4415	3942	3515	3126	41
42	1.5351	1.1498	0.9488	8120	7081	6243	5541	4937	4407	3934	3508	3120	42
43	1.5249	1.1455	0.9462	8101	7066	6231	5531	4928	4399	3927	3501	3114	43
44	1.5149	1.1413	0.9435	8081	7050	6218	5520	4918	4390	3919	3495	3108	44
45	1.5051	1.1372	0.9409	8062	7035	6205	5509	4909	4382	3912	3488	3102	45
46	1.4956	1.1331	0.9383	8043	7020	6193	5498	4900	4374	3905	3481	3096	46
47	1.4863	1.1290	0.9356	8023	7005	6180	5488	4890	4365	3897	3475	3089	47
48	1.4771	1.1249	0.9330	8004	6990	6168	5477	4881	4357	3890	3468	3083	48
49	1.4682	1.1209	0.9304	7985	6975	6155	5466	4872	4349	3882	3461	3077	49
50	1.4594	1.1170	0.9279	7966	6960	6143	5456	4863	4341	3875	3455	3071	50
51	1.4508	1.1130	0.9254	7947	6945	6131	5445	4853	4333	3868	3448	3065	51
52	1.4424	1.1091	0.9228	7929	6930	6118	5435	4844	4324	3860	3441	3059	52
53	1.4341	1.1053	0.9203	7910	6915	6106	5424	4835	4316	3853	3435	3053	53
54	1.4260	1.1015	0.9178	7891	6900	6094	5414	4826	4308	3846	3428	3047	54
55	1.4180	1.0977	0.9153	7873	6885	6081	5403	4817	4300	3838	3421	3041	55
56	1.4102	1.0939	0.9128	7854	6871	6069	5393	4808	4292	3831	3415	3035	56
57	1.4025	1.0902	0.9104	7836	6856	6057	5382	4799	4284	3824	3408	3028	57
58	1.3949	1.0865	0.9079	7818	6841	6045	5372	4789	4276	3817	3401	3022	58
59	1.3875	1.0828	0.9055	7800	6827	6033	5361	4780	4268	3809	3395	3016	59
	0	1	2	3	4	5	6	7	8	9	10	11	

Minutes may be substituted for Degrees or Hours, and Seconds substituted for minutes as required for use in figuring house cusps using logarithms.

Min.	TABLE OF PROPORTIONAL LOGARITHMS												Min.
	Hours or Degrees												
	12	13	14	15	16	17	18	19	20	21	22	23	
0	3010	2663	2341	2041	1761	1498	1249	1015	0792	0580	0378	0185	0
1	3004	2657	2336	2036	1756	1493	1245	1011	0788	0577	0375	0182	1
2	2998	2652	2330	2032	1752	1489	1241	1007	0785	0573	0371	0179	2
3	2992	2646	2325	2027	1747	1485	1237	1003	0781	0570	0368	0175	3
4	2986	2641	2320	2022	1743	1481	1234	0999	0777	0566	0364	0172	4
5	2980	2635	2315	2017	1738	1476	1229	0996	0774	0563	0361	0169	5
6	2974	2629	2310	2012	1734	1472	1225	0992	0770	0559	0358	0166	6
7	2968	2624	2305	2008	1729	1468	1221	0988	0766	0556	0355	0163	7
8	2962	2618	2300	2003	1725	1464	1217	0984	0763	0552	0352	0160	8
9	2956	2613	2295	1998	1720	1460	1213	0980	0759	0549	0348	0157	9
10	2950	2607	2289	1993	1716	1455	1209	0977	0756	0546	0345	0153	10
11	2945	2602	2284	1989	1711	1451	1205	0973	0752	0542	0342	0150	11
12	2938	2596	2279	1984	1707	1447	1201	0969	0749	0539	0339	0147	12
13	2933	2591	2274	1979	1702	1443	1197	0965	0745	0535	0335	0144	13
14	2927	2585	2269	1974	1698	1438	1193	0962	0742	0532	0332	0141	14
15	2921	2580	2264	1969	1694	1434	1189	0958	0738	0529	0329	0138	15
16	2915	2575	2259	1965	1689	1430	1185	0954	0734	0525	0326	0135	16
17	2909	2569	2254	1960	1685	1426	1182	0950	0731	0522	0322	0132	17
18	2903	2564	2249	1955	1680	1422	1178	0947	0727	0518	0319	0129	18
19	2897	2558	2244	1950	1676	1417	1174	0943	0724	0515	0316	0125	19
20	2891	2553	2239	1946	1671	1413	1170	0939	0720	0511	0313	0122	20
21	2885	2547	2234	1941	1667	1409	1166	0935	0717	0508	0309	0119	21
22	2880	2542	2229	1936	1663	1405	1162	0932	0713	0505	0306	0116	22
23	2874	2536	2223	1932	1658	1401	1158	0928	0709	0501	0303	0113	23
24	2868	2531	2218	1927	1654	1397	1154	0924	0706	0498	0300	0110	24
25	2862	2526	2213	1922	1649	1393	1150	0920	0702	0495	0296	0107	25
26	2856	2520	2208	1917	1645	1388	1146	0917	0699	0491	0292	0104	26
27	2850	2515	2203	1913	1640	1384	1142	0913	0695	0488	0290	0101	27
28	2845	2509	2198	1908	1636	1380	1138	0909	0692	0485	0287	0098	28
29	2839	2504	2193	1903	1632	1376	1134	0905	0688	0481	0283	0094	29
30	2833	2499	2188	1899	1627	1372	1130	0902	0685	0478	0280	0091	30
31	2827	2493	2183	1894	1623	1368	1126	0898	0681	0474	0277	0088	31
32	2821	2488	2178	1890	1619	1363	1123	0894	0678	0471	0274	0085	32
33	2816	2483	2173	1885	1614	1359	1118	0891	0674	0468	0271	0082	33
34	2810	2477	2168	1880	1610	1355	1115	0887	0670	0464	0267	0079	34
35	2804	2472	2164	1875	1605	1351	1111	0883	0667	0461	0264	0076	35
36	2798	2467	2159	1871	1601	1347	1107	0880	0664	0458	0261	0073	36
37	2793	2461	2154	1866	1597	1343	1103	0876	0660	0454	0258	0070	37
38	2787	2456	2149	1862	1592	1339	1099	0872	0656	0451	0255	0067	38
39	2781	2451	2144	1857	1588	1335	1095	0868	0653	0448	0251	0064	39
40	2775	2445	2139	1852	1584	1331	1092	0865	0649	0444	0248	0061	40
41	2770	2440	2134	1848	1579	1327	1088	0861	0646	0441	0245	0058	41
42	2764	2435	2129	1843	1575	1322	1084	0857	0642	0437	0242	0055	42
43	2758	2430	2124	1838	1571	1318	1080	0854	0639	0434	0239	0052	43
44	2753	2424	2119	1834	1566	1314	1076	0850	0635	0431	0235	0048	44
45	2747	2419	2114	1829	1562	1310	1072	0846	0632	0428	0232	0045	45
46	2741	2414	2109	1825	1558	1306	1068	0843	0629	0424	0229	0042	46
47	2736	2409	2104	1820	1553	1302	1064	0839	0625	0421	0226	0039	47
48	2730	2403	2099	1816	1549	1298	1061	0835	0621	0418	0223	0036	48
49	2724	2398	2095	1811	1545	1294	1057	0832	0618	0414	0220	0033	49
50	2719	2393	2090	1806	1540	1290	1053	0828	0614	0411	0216	0030	50
51	2713	2388	2085	1802	1536	1286	1049	0824	0611	0408	0213	0027	51
52	2707	2382	2080	1797	1532	1282	1045	0821	0608	0404	0210	0024	52
53	2702	2377	2075	1793	1528	1278	1041	0817	0604	0401	0207	0021	53
54	2696	2372	2070	1788	1523	1274	1037	0814	0601	0398	0204	0018	54
55	2691	2367	2065	1784	1519	1270	1034	0810	0597	0394	0201	0015	55
56	2685	2362	2061	1779	1515	1266	1030	0806	0594	0391	0197	0012	56
57	2679	2356	2056	1774	1510	1261	1026	0803	0590	0388	0194	0009	57
58	2674	2351	2051	1770	1506	1257	1022	0799	0587	0384	0191	0006	58
59	2668	2346	2046	1765	1502	1253	1018	0795	0583	0381	0188	0003	59
	12	13	14	15	16	17	18	19	20	21	22	23	

APPENDIX I
LATITUDE AND LONGITUDE OF VARIOUS CITIES

	LAT.	LONG.
AKRON	41N05	81W31
ALGIERS	36N48	3E21
AMSTERDAM	52N23	4E53
ANKARA	39N57	32E50
ANTWERP	51N13	4E25
ATHENS	37N58	23E43
ATLANTA	33N46	84W23
BALTIMORE	39N19	76W37
BANKOK	13N45	100E31
BARCELONA	41N22	2E10
BEIRUT	33N54	35E28
BELGRADE	44N50	20E27
BERGEN	60N24	5E18
BERLIN	52N30	13E25
BERN	46N57	7E26
BIRMINGHAM	33N31	86W49
BOGOTA	4N40	74W05
BOMBAY	19N57	72E50
BOSTON	42N22	71W04
BRISBANE	27S28	153E02
BRUSSELS	50N51	4E22
BUCHAREST	44N26	26E06
BUDAPEST	47N30	19E04
BUENOS AIRES	34S36	58W27
BUFFALO	42N53	78W52
CAIRO	30N03	31E15
CARACAS	10N30	66W55
CARDIFF	51N29	3W10
CHICAGO	41N52	87W39
CINCINNATI	39N06	84W31
CLEVELAND	41N30	81W43
COLUMBUS	39N38	83W01

COPENHAGEN	55N41	12E35
DALLAS	32N47	96W47
DENVER	39N45	104W59
DETROIT	42N20	83W03
DUBLIN	53N23	6W20
EL PASO	31N45	106W29
FORT WORTH	32N45	97W20
FRANKFURT	50N07	8E41
GENEVA	46N12	6E09
GLASGOW	55N53	4W15
HAVANA	23N08	82W24
HAMBURG	53N33	9E58
HELSINKI	60N10	24E57
HONG KONG	22N18	114E11
HONOLULU	21N19	157W52
HOUSTON	29N45	95W23
INDIANAPOLIS	39N46	86W10
JERSEY CITY	40N43	74W02
JERUSALEM	31N47	35E10
KANSAS CITY	39N07	94W38
LANCESTER	53N03	2W48
LA PAZ	16S30	68W09
LE HAVRE	49N29	0E07
LEIPZIG	51N20	12E24
LENINGRAD	59N57	30E18
LIMA	12S03	77W03
LISBON	38N43	9W11
LONDON	51N31	0W06
LONG BEACH	33N46	118W11
LOS ANGELES	34N03	118W15
LOUISVILLE	38N15	85W45
LUCERN	47N03	8E18
LUXEMBURG	49N38	6E10
MADRID	40N25	3W41
MANILA	14N35	120E59
MECCA	21N26	39E49
MELBOURNE	37S50	145E00
MEMPHIS	35N09	90W03
MEXICO CITY	19N26	99W07
MIAMI	25N47	80W11

MILWAUKEE	43N02	87W55
MINNEAPOLIS	44N59	93W16
MOBILE	30N42	88W02
MONTEVIDEO	34S53	56W10
MOSCOW	55N45	37E34
NAGOYA	35N08	136E55
NEWARK	40N44	74W11
NEW ORLEANS	29N58	90W04
NEW YORK CITY	40N45	73W57
OAKLAND	37N48	122W16
OMAHA	41N15	95W57
OSAKA	34N39	135E29
OSLO	59N55	10E44
PANAMA CITY	8N57	79W32
PARIS	48N50	2E20
PEKING	39N36	126E24
PHILADELPHIA	39N57	75W11
PHOENIX	33N27	112W04
PITTSBURGH	40N27	80W00
PORTLAND	45N31	122W41
PRAGUE	50N05	14E25
QUEBEC	46N48	71W13
REYKJAVIK	64N09	21W55
RIGA	56N57	24E07
RIO DE JANERO	22S54	43W15
ROCHESTER	43N10	77W37
ROME	41N54	12E29
ROTTERDAM	51N55	4E30
SACRAMENTO	38N35	121W30
ST LOUIS	38N38	90W12
ST PAUL	44N57	93W06
SALT LAKE CITY	40N46	111W54
SAN ANTONIO	29N25	98W29
SAN DIEGO	32N43	117W10
SAN FRANCISCO	37N47	122W26
SANTIAGO	33S27	70W40
SAN JUAN	18N28	66W07
SEATTLE	47N37	122W20
SEOUL	37N32	126E57
SHANGHAI	31N14	121E30

SHREVEPORT	32N31	93W45
SINGAPORE	1N16	103E51
STOCKHOLM	59N21	18E04
SYDNEY	33S55	151E10
TAMPA	27N57	82W27
TANGIER	35N47	5W48
TEHERAN	35N40	51E26
TOKYO	35N40	139E45
TOLEDO	41N39	83W33
TORONTO	43N39	79W22
TULSA	36N09	96W00
VIENNA	48N13	16E23
WARSAW	52N13	21E02
WASHINGTON, D.C.	38N53	77W00
WICHITA	37N42	97W20
YOKOHAMA	35N25	139E38
ZURICH	47N23	8E33

APPENDIX J
PLUTO EPHEMERIS: 1900 TO 1960

1900	LONG	DEC	1900	LONG	DEC
	GEMINI	NORTH		GEMINI	NORTH
Jan 1	15 15R	12 55	Jun 30	16 41D	13 33
Jan 11	15 5	12 56	Jul 10	16 54	13 33
Jan 21	14 57	12 57	Jul 20	17 6	13 33
Jan 31	14 50	12 58	Jul 30	17 16	13 34
Feb 10	14 45	13 0	Aug 9	17 25	13 33
Feb 20	14 42	13 2	Aug 19	17 32	13 32
Mar 2	14 42D	13 4	Aug 29	17 38	13 32
Mar 12	14 43	13 7	Sep 8	17 41	13 30
Mar 22	14 47	13 10	Sep 18	17 42R	13 28
Apr 1	14 53	13 12	Sep 28	17 41	13 27
Apr 11	15 1	13 15	Oct 8	17 37	13 25
Apr 21	15 10	13 18	Oct 18	17 32	13 23
May 1	15 21	13 21	Oct 28	17 25	13 22
May 11	15 34	13 24	Nov 7	17 16	13 20
May 21	15 47	13 26	Nov 17	17 6	13 19
May 31	16 0	13 28	Nov 27	16 55	13 17
Jun 10	16 14	13 30	Dec 7	16 44	13 17
Jun 20	16 28	13 31	Dec 17	16 32	13 16
			Dec 27	16 21	13 16

1901		LONG	DEC	1902		LONG	DEC
		GEMINI	NORTH			GEMINI	NORTH
Jan	6	16 10R	13 16	Jan	1	17 17R	13 37
Jan	16	16 1	13 17	Jan	11	17 6	13 37
Jan	26	15 53	13 18	Jan	21	16 58	13 38
Feb	5	15 47	13 20	Jan	31	16 50	13 40
Feb	15	15 43	13 21	Feb	10	16 45	13 41
Feb	25	15 41	13 23	Feb	20	16 42	13 43
Mar	7	15 41D	13 26	Mar	2	16 41D	13 45
Mar	17	15 44	13 29	Mar	12	16 42	13 48
Mar	27	15 48	13 31	Mar	22	16 45	13 50
Apr	6	15 55	13 34	Apr	1	16 50	13 53
Apr	16	16 4	13 37	Apr	11	16 58	13 56
Apr	26	16 14	13 40	Apr	21	17 7	13 59
May	6	16 25	13 42	May	1	17 18	14 1
May	16	16 38	13 45	May	11	17 30	14 4
May	26	16 51	13 47	May	21	17 43	14 6
Jun	5	17 5	13 49	May	31	17 56	14 8
Jun	15	17 19	13 51	Jun	10	18 10	14 10
Jun	25	17 33	13 52	Jun	20	18 24	14 11
Jul	5	17 46	13 53	Jun	30	18 38	14 12
Jul	15	17 58	13 53	Jul	10	18 51	14 13
Jul	25	18 10	13 54	Jul	20	19 3	14 14
Aug	4	18 20	13 53	Jul	30	19 14	14 13
Aug	14	18 28	13 53	Aug	9	19 23	14 13
Aug	24	18 34	13 52	Aug	19	19 31	14 13
Sep	3	18 39	13 51	Aug	29	19 36	14 11
Sep	13	18 41	13 49	Sep	8	19 40	14 10
Sep	23	18 41R	13 48	Sep	18	19 42	14 9
Oct	3	18 39	13 46	Sep	28	19 41R	14 7
Oct	13	18 35	13 45	Oct	8	19 38	14 6
Oct	23	18 29	13 43	Oct	18	19 33	14 4
Nov	2	18 22	13 41	Oct	28	19 27	14 3
Nov	12	18 12	13 40	Nov	7	19 18	14 1
Nov	22	18 2	13 38	Nov	17	19 9	14 0
Dec	2	17 51	13 38	Nov	27	18 58	13 59
Dec	12	17 39	13 37	Dec	7	18 46	13 58
Dec	22	17 28	13 36	Dec	17	18 35	13 57
Jan	1	17 17	13 37	Dec	27	18 23	13 58

1903	LONG	DEC	1904	LONG	DEC
	GEMINI	NORTH		GEMINI	NORTH
Jan 6	18 13R	13 58	Jan 1	19 20R	14 18
Jan 16	18 3	13 58	Jan 11	19 9	14 18
Jan 26	17 55	14 0	Jan 21	19 0	14 20
Feb 5	17 48	14 1	Jan 31	18 52	14 21
Feb 15	17 43	14 2	Feb 10	18 46	14 22
Feb 25	17 41	14 5	Feb 20	18 43	14 24
Mar 7	17 41D	14 7	Mar 1	18 41	14 26
Mar 17	17 43	14 9	Mar 11	18 41D	14 29
Mar 27	17 47	14 12	Mar 21	18 44	14 31
Apr 6	17 53	14 15	Mar 31	18 49	14 34
Apr 16	18 1	14 18	Apr 10	18 56	14 36
Apr 26	18 11	14 20	Apr 20	19 5	14 39
May 6	18 22	14 23	Apr 30	19 15	14 41
May 16	18 34	14 25	May 10	19 27	14 44
May 26	18 48	14 27	May 20	19 40	14 46
Jun 5	19 1	14 29	May 30	19 53	14 48
Jun 15	19 15	14 31	Jun 9	20 7	14 50
Jun 25	19 29	14 31	Jun 19	20 21	14 51
Jul 5	19 43	14 32	Jun 29	20 35	14 52
Jul 15	19 56	14 33	Jul 9	20 48	14 53
Jul 25	20 7	14 33	Jul 19	21 1	14 53
Aug 4	20 18	14 33	Jul 29	21 12	14 53
Aug 14	20 26	14 33	Aug 8	21 22	14 53
Aug 24	20 33	14 32	Aug 18	21 30	14 52
Sep 3	20 38	14 31	Aug 28	21 36	14 51
Sep 13	20 41	14 30	Sep 7	21 41	14 50
Sep 23	20 42R	14 28	Sep 17	21 43	14 49
Oct 3	20 41	14 27	Sep 27	21 43R	14 47
Oct 13	20 37	14 25	Oct 7	21 41	14 46
Oct 23	20 32	14 24	Oct 17	21 36	14 44
Nov 2	20 24	14 22	Oct 27	21 30	14 43
Nov 12	20 15	14 21	Nov 6	21 22	14 42
Nov 22	20 5	14 20	Nov 16	21 13	14 41
Dec 2	19 54	14 19	Nov 26	21 2	14 40
Dec 12	19 42	14 18	Dec 6	20 51	14 39
Dec 22	19 31	14 18	Dec 16	20 39	14 39
Jan 1	19 20	14 18	Dec 26	20 27	14 39

1905	LONG	DEC	1906	LONG	DEC
	GEMINI	NORTH		GEMINI	NORTH
Jan 5	20 16R	14 39	Jan 10	21 14R	15 0
Jan 15	20 6	14 40	Jan 20	21 4	15 0
Jan 25	19 58	14 41	Jan 30	20 56	15 1
Feb 4	19 51	14 42	Feb 9	20 50	15 3
Feb 14	19 45	14 44	Feb 19	20 45	15 5
Feb 24	19 42	14 46	Mar 1	20 43	15 7
Mar 6	19 41D	14 48	Mar 11	20 43D	15 9
Mar 16	19 43	14 50	Mar 21	20 45	15 11
Mar 26	19 47	14 53	Mar 31	20 50	15 14
Apr 5	19 52	14 55	Apr 10	20 56	15 16
Apr 15	20 0	14 57	Apr 20	21 4	15 19
Apr 25	20 9	15 0	Apr 30	21 15	15 21
May 5	20 20	15 2	May 10	21 26	15 23
May 15	20 33	15 4	May 20	21 39	15 25
May 25	20 46	15 6	May 30	21 52	15 27
Jun 4	20 59	15 8	Jun 9	22 6	15 28
Jun 14	21 15	15 9	Jun 19	22 20	15 29
Jun 24	21 28	15 11	Jun 29	22 34	15 31
Jul 4	21 41	15 12	Jul 9	22 48	15 31
Jul 14	21 54	15 12	Jul 19	23 0	15 31
Jul 24	22 6	15 12	Jul 29	23 12	15 32
Aug 3	22 17	15 12	Aug 8	23 22	15 31
Aug 13	22 26	15 11	Aug 18	23 31	15 30
Aug 23	22 34	15 11	Aug 28	23 38	15 30
Sep 2	22 39	15 10	Sep 7	23 43	15 29
Sep 12	22 43	15 9	Sep 17	23 46	15 28
Sep 22	22 44	15 8	Sep 27	23 46R	15 27
Oct 2	22 44R	15 6	Oct 7	23 44	15 25
Oct 12	22 41	15 5	Oct 17	23 41	15 24
Oct 22	22 36	15 4	Oct 27	23 35	15 23
Nov 1	22 29	15 2	Nov 6	23 27	15 22
Nov 11	22 20	15 1	Nov 16	23 18	15 21
Nov 21	22 10	15 0	Nov 26	23 8	15 20
Dec 1	21 59	14 59	Dec 6	22 56	15 19
Dec 11	21 47	14 59	Dec 16	22 45	15 19
Dec 21	21 36	14 59	Dec 26	22 33	15 19
Dec 31	21 24	14 59	Jan 5	22 22	15 19

1907	LONG	DEC	1908	LONG	DEC
	GEMINI	NORTH		GEMINI	NORTH
Jan 5	22 22R	15 19	Jan 10	23 20R	15 40
Jan 15	22 11	15 20	Jan 20	23 10	15 40
Jan 25	22 2	15 21	Jan 30	23 1	15 42
Feb 4	21 55	15 22	Feb 9	22 54	15 43
Feb 14	21 49	15 24	Feb 19	22 49	15 45
Feb 24	21 46	15 26	Feb 29	22 47	15 47
Mar 6	21 44	15 28	Mar 10	22 46D	15 49
Mar 16	21 45D	15 30	Mar 20	22 48	15 51
Mar 26	21 48	15 32	Mar 30	22 52	15 53
Apr 5	21 53	15 35	Apr 9	22 58	15 56
Apr 15	22 1	15 37	Apr 19	23 6	15 58
Apr 25	22 10	15 39	Apr 29	23 15	16 0
May 5	22 20	15 41	May 9	23 27	16 2
May 15	22 32	15 43	May 19	23 39	16 4
May 25	22 45	15 45	May 29	23 52	16 5
Jun 4	22 59	15 47	Jun 8	24 6	16 7
Jun 14	23 13	15 48	Jun 18	24 20	16 8
Jun 24	23 27	15 49	Jun 28	24 35	16 9
Jul 4	23 41	15 50	Jul 8	24 48	16 9
Jul 14	23 54	15 50	Jul 18	25 1	16 10
Jul 24	24 7	15 51	Jul 28	25 14	16 9
Aug 3	24 18	15 50	Aug 7	25 24	16 9
Aug 13	24 28	15 50	Aug 17	25 33	16 9
Aug 23	24 36	15 50	Aug 27	25 41	16 8
Sep 2	24 42	15 48	Sep 6	25 46	16 7
Sep 12	24 46	15 47	Sep 16	25 50	16 6
Sep 22	24 48	15 46	Sep 26	25 51R	16 5
Oct 2	24 48R	15 45	Oct 6	25 50	16 4
Oct 12	24 45	15 44	Oct 16	25 46	16 3
Oct 22	24 41	15 43	Oct 26	25 41	16 2
Nov 1	24 34	15 42	Nov 5	25 34	16 1
Nov 11	24 26	15 41	Nov 15	25 25	16 0
Nov 21	24 16	15 40	Nov 25	25 15	15 59
Dec 1	24 6	15 39	Dec 5	25 4	15 59
Dec 11	23 54	15 39	Dec 15	24 52	15 58
Dec 21	23 42	15 39	Dec 25	24 40	15 59
Dec 31	23 31	15 39	Jan 4	24 29	15 59

1909	LONG	DEC	1910	LONG	DEC
	GEMINI	NORTH		GEMINI	NORTH
Jan 4	24 29R	15 59	Jan 9	25 27R	16 19
Jan 14	24 18	16 0	Jan 19	25 17	16 20
Jan 24	24 9	16 1	Jan 29	25 8	16 21
Feb 3	24 1	16 2	Feb 8	25 1	16 22
Feb 13	23 54	16 4	Feb 18	24 55	16 24
Feb 23	23 50	16 6	Feb 28	24 52	16 26
Mar 5	23 48	16 8	Mar 10	24 51D	16 28
Mar 15	23 49D	16 9	Mar 20	24 52	16 30
Mar 25	23 51	16 12	Mar 30	24 55	16 32
Apr 4	23 56	16 14	Apr 9	25 1	16 34
Apr 14	24 3	16 16	Apr 19	25 8	16 36
Apr 24	24 11	16 18	Apr 29	25 18	16 38
May 4	24 22	16 20	May 9	25 29	16 40
May 14	24 33	16 22	May 19	25 41	16 42
May 24	24 46	16 24	May 29	25 54	16 43
Jun 3	25 0	16 25	Jun 8	26 8	16 45
Jun 13	25 14	16 26	Jun 18	26 22	16 45
Jun 23	25 28	16 27	Jun 28	26 36	16 46
Jul 3	25 43	16 28	Jul 8	26 50	16 47
Jul 13	25 56	16 28	Jul 18	27 4	16 47
Jul 23	26 9	16 28	Jul 28	27 16	16 47
Aug 2	26 20	16 28	Aug 7	27 27	16 47
Aug 12	26 31	16 28	Aug 17	27 37	16 46
Aug 22	26 39	16 27	Aug 27	27 45	16 45
Sep 1	26 46	16 26	Sep 6	27 51	16 45
Sep 11	26 51	16 25	Sep 16	27 55	16 44
Sep 21	26 53	16 24	Sep 26	27 57	16 43
Oct 1	26 54R	16 23	Oct 6	27 56R	16 42
Oct 11	26 52	16 22	Oct 16	27 54	16 41
Oct 21	26 48	16 21	Oct 26	27 49	16 40
Oct 31	26 41	16 20	Nov 5	27 42	16 39
Nov 10	26 34	16 19	Nov 15	27 33	16 38
Nov 20	26 24	16 19	Nov 25	27 23	16 38
Nov 30	26 14	16 18	Dec 5	27 12	16 37
Dec 10	26 2	16 18	Dec 15	27 1	16 38
Dec 20	25 50	16 18	Dec 25	26 49	16 38
Dec 30	25 39	16 19	Jan 4	26 37	16 38

1911	LONG	DEC	1912	LONG	DEC
	GEMINI	NORTH		GEMINI	NORTH
Jan 4	26 37R	16 38	Jan 9	27 36R	16 58
Jan 14	26 26	16 39	Jan 19	27 26	16 59
Jan 24	26 16	16 40	Jan 29	27 16	17 0
Feb 3	26 8	16 41	Feb 8	27 8	17 1
Feb 13	26 1	16 43	Feb 18	27 2	17 3
Feb 23	25 56	16 45	Feb 28	26 58	17 5
Mar 5	25 54	16 46	Mar 9	26 57	17 7
Mar 15	25 54D	16 48	Mar 19	26 57D	17 8
Mar 25	25 56	16 50	Mar 29	27 0	17 10
Apr 4	26 0	16 52	Apr 8	27 5	17 12
Apr 14	26 6	16 54	Apr 18	27 12	17 14
Apr 24	26 14	16 56	Apr 28	27 21	17 16
May 4	26 24	16 58	May 8	27 32	17 18
May 14	26 36	17 0	May 18	27 44	17 19
May 24	26 49	17 1	May 28	27 57	17 21
Jun 3	27 2	17 3	Jun 7	28 11	17 21
Jun 13	27 16	17 3	Jun 17	28 25	17 22
Jun 23	27 31	17 4	Jun 27	28 39	17 23
Jul 3	27 45	17 5	Jul 7	28 54	17 23
Jul 13	27 59	17 5	Jul 17	29 7	17 23
Jul 23	28 12	17 5	Jul 27	29 20	17 23
Aug 2	28 24	17 5	Aug 6	29 32	17 23
Aug 12	28 35	17 5	Aug 16	29 42	17 22
Aug 22	28 44	17 4	Aug 26	29 50	17 22
Sep 1	28 51	17 3	Sep 5	29 57	17 21
Sep 11	28 56	17 2		CANCER	
Sep 21	28 59	17 2	Sep 15	0 2	17 20
Oct 1	29 0R	17 1	Sep 25	0 4	17 19
Oct 11	28 59	17 0	Oct 5	0 4R	17 19
Oct 21	28 56	16 59	Oct 15	0 2	17 18
Oct 31	28 50	16 58		GEMINI	
Nov 10	28 43	16 57	Oct 25	29 58	17 17
Nov 20	28 33	16 57	Nov 4	29 51	17 16
Nov 30	28 23	16 57	Nov 14	29 43	17 16
Dec 10	28 12	16 57	Nov 24	29 34	17 15
Dec 20	28 0	16 57	Dec 4	29 23	17 16
Dec 30	27 48	16 57	Dec 14	29 11	17 16
			Dec 24	28 59	17 16
			Jan 3	28 47	17 17

1913	LONG	DEC	1914	LONG	DEC
	GEMINI	NORTH		GEMINI	NORTH
Jan 3	28 47R	17 17	Jan 8	29 47R	17 36
Jan 13	28 36	17 18	Jan 18	29 36	17 37
Jan 23	28 26	17 18	Jan 28	29 26	17 38
Feb 2	28 17	17 20	Feb 7	29 18	17 39
Feb 12	28 10	17 21	Feb 17	29 12	17 41
Feb 22	28 4	17 23	Feb 27	29 7	17 43
Mar 4	28 1	17 25	Mar 9	29 5	17 44
Mar 14	28 0D	17 26	Mar 19	29 5D	17 46
Mar 24	28 2	17 28	Mar 29	29 7	17 48
Apr 3	28 5	17 30	Apr 8	29 11	17 50
Apr 13	28 11	17 32	Apr 18	29 18	17 51
Apr 23	28 19	17 34	Apr 28	29 27	17 53
May 3	28 29	17 35	May 8	29 37	17 54
May 13	28 40	17 37	May 18	29 49	17 56
May 23	28 52	17 38		CANCER	
Jun 2	29 6	17 39	May 28	0 2	17 57
Jun 12	29 20	17 40	Jun 7	0 15	17 57
Jun 22	29 34	17 41	Jun 17	0 30	17 59
Jul 2	29 49	17 41	Jun 27	0 44	17 59
	CANCER		Jul 7	0 59	17 59
Jul 12	0 3	17 41	Jul 17	1 12	17 59
Jul 22	0 16	17 41	Jul 27	1 26	17 59
Aug 1	0 29	17 41	Aug 6	1 38	17 59
Aug 11	0 40	17 41	Aug 16	1 48	17 58
Aug 21	0 50	17 40	Aug 26	1 58	17 57
Aug 31	0 58	17 39	Sep 5	2 5	17 57
Sep 10	1 3	17 39	Sep 15	2 10	17 56
Sep 20	1 7	17 38	Sep 25	2 13	17 55
Sep 30	1 9	17 37	Oct 5	2 14R	17 55
Oct 10	1 8R	17 36	Oct 15	2 12	17 54
Oct 20	1 5	17 35	Oct 25	2 8	17 53
Oct 30	1 0	17 35	Nov 4	2 2	17 53
Nov 9	0 53	17 35	Nov 14	1 55	17 52
Nov 19	0 44	17 34	Nov 24	1 45	17 53
Nov 29	0 34	17 34	Dec 4	1 35	17 53
Dec 9	0 23	17 34	Dec 14	1 23	17 53
Dec 19	0 11	17 34	Dec 24	1 11	17 53
	GEMINI		Jan 3	0 59	17 54
Dec 29	29 59	17 35			

1915		LONG	DEC	1916		LONG	DEC
		CANCER	NORTH			CANCER	NORTH
Jan	3	0 59R	17 54	Jan	8	2 0R	18 13
Jan	13	0 48	17 55	Jan	18	1 49	18 14
Jan	23	0 37	17 56	Jan	28	1 39	18 15
Feb	2	0 28	17 57	Feb	7	1 30	18 17
Feb	12	0 20	17 59	Feb	17	1 23	18 18
Feb	22	0 14	18 0	Feb	27	1 18	18 20
Mar	4	0 10	18 2	Mar	8	1 15	18 21
Mar	14	0 9	18 4	Mar	18	1 14D	18 23
Mar	24	0 10D	18 6	Mar	28	1 16	18 25
Apr	3	0 13	18 7	Apr	7	1 20	18 26
Apr	13	0 18	18 9	Apr	17	1 26	18 28
Apr	23	0 26	18 10	Apr	27	1 34	18 29
May	3	0 35	18 12	May	7	1 44	18 31
May	13	0 46	18 13	May	17	1 55	18 31
May	23	0 58	18 14	May	27	2 8	18 32
Jun	2	1 11	18 15	Jun	6	2 22	18 33
Jun	12	1 25	18 16	Jun	16	2 36	18 34
Jun	22	1 40	18 16	Jun	26	2 51	18 34
Jul	2	1 54	18 17	Jul	6	3 5	18 34
Jul	12	2 9	18 17	Jul	16	3 20	18 34
Jul	22	2 23	18 17	Jul	26	3 33	18 34
Aug	1	2 35	18 16	Aug	5	3 46	18 33
Aug	11	2 47	18 16	Aug	15	3 57	18 33
Aug	21	2 57	18 15	Aug	25	4 7	18 32
Aug	31	3 6	18 15	Sep	4	4 14	18 31
Sep	10	3 12	18 14	Sep	14	4 20	18 31
Sep	20	3 17	18 13	Sep	24	4 24	18 30
Sep	30	3 19	18 12	Oct	4	4 25	18 29
Oct	10	3 19R	18 12	Oct	14	4 24R	18 29
Oct	20	3 16	18 11	Oct	24	4 21	18 28
Oct	30	3 12	18 11	Nov	3	4 16	18 28
Nov	9	3 5	18 10	Nov	13	4 8	18 28
Nov	19	2 57	18 10	Nov	23	3 59	18 28
Nov	29	2 47	18 11	Dec	3	3 49	18 28
Dec	9	2 36	18 11	Dec	13	3 38	18 29
Dec	19	2 24	18 11	Dec	23	3 26	18 30
Dec	29	2 12	18 12	Jan	2	3 14	18 30

1917	LONG	DEC	1918	LONG	DEC
	CANCER	NORTH		CANCER	NORTH
Jan 2	3 14R	18 30	Jan 7	4 16R	18 49
Jan 12	3 2	18 32	Jan 17	4 4	18 50
Jan 22	2 51	18 33	Jan 27	3 53	18 51
Feb 1	2 41	18 34	Feb 6	3 44	18 53
Feb 11	2 33	18 36	Feb 16	3 37	18 54
Feb 21	2 26	18 37	Feb 26	3 31	18 56
Mar 3	2 22	18 39	Mar 8	3 27	18 57
Mar 13	2 20	18 40	Mar 18	3 26D	18 59
Mar 23	2 20D	18 42	Mar 28	3 27	19 1
Apr 2	2 23	18 44	Apr 7	3 31	19 2
Apr 12	2 28	18 45	Apr 17	3 36	19 3
Apr 22	2 34	18 46	Apr 27	3 44	19 5
May 2	2 43	18 48	May 7	3 53	19 5
May 12	2 54	18 49	May 17	4 5	19 6
May 22	3 6	18 49	May 27	4 17	19 7
Jun 1	3 19	18 50	Jun 6	4 31	19 8
Jun 11	3 33	18 51	Jun 16	4 45	19 8
Jun 21	3 48	18 51	Jun 26	5 0	19 8
Jul 1	4 2	18 51	Jul 6	5 14	19 8
Jul 11	4 17	18 51	Jul 16	5 29	19 8
Jul 21	4 31	18 51	Jul 26	5 43	19 7
Jul 31	4 44	18 51	Aug 5	5 56	19 7
Aug 10	4 56	18 50	Aug 15	6 7	19 6
Aug 20	5 7	18 49	Aug 25	6 18	19 6
Aug 30	5 16	18 49	Sep 4	6 26	19 5
Sep 9	5 23	18 48	Sep 14	6 33	19 4
Sep 19	5 28	18 47	Sep 24	6 37	19 4
Sep 29	5 31	18 47	Oct 4	6 39	19 3
Oct 9	5 32R	18 46	Oct 14	6 39R	19 3
Oct 19	5 30	18 46	Oct 24	6 36	19 2
Oct 29	5 26	18 45	Nov 3	6 31	19 2
Nov 8	5 20	18 34	Nov 13	6 24	19 2
Nov 18	5 12	18 46	Nov 23	6 16	19 3
Nov 28	5 2	18 46	Dec 3	6 6	19 3
Dec 8	4 52	18 46	Dec 13	5 54	19 4
Dec 18	4 40	18 47	Dec 23	5 43	19 5
Dec 28	4 28	18 48	Jan 2	5 30	19 6

1919	LONG	DEC	1920	LONG	DEC
	CANCER	NORTH		CANCER	NORTH
Jan 2	5 30R	19 6	Jan 7	6 33R	19 24
Jan 12	5 18	19 7	Jan 17	6 22	19 25
Jan 22	5 7	19 8	Jan 27	6 11	19 26
Feb 1	4 57	19 10	Feb 6	6 1	19 28
Feb 11	4 48	19 11	Feb 16	5 53	19 29
Feb 21	4 41	19 13	Feb 26	5 46	19 31
Mar 3	4 36	19 14	Mar 7	5 42	19 32
Mar 13	4 33	19 16	Mar 17	5 40	19 34
Mar 23	4 33D	19 17	Mar 27	5 41D	19 35
Apr 2	4 35	19 19	Apr 6	5 44	19 36
Apr 12	4 39	19 20	Apr 16	5 49	19 38
Apr 22	4 46	19 21	Apr 26	5 56	19 39
May 2	4 54	19 22	May 6	6 5	19 39
May 12	5 4	19 23	May 16	6 16	19 40
May 22	5 16	19 24	May 26	6 28	19 41
Jun 1	5 29	19 24	Jun 5	6 42	19 41
Jun 11	5 43	19 24	Jun 15	6 56	19 41
Jun 21	5 57	19 25	Jun 25	7 11	19 41
Jul 1	6 12	19 25	Jul 5	7 25	19 41
Jul 11	6 27	19 24	Jul 15	7 40	19 40
Jul 21	6 41	19 24	Jul 25	7 54	19 40
Jul 31	6 55	19 23	Aug 4	8 8	19 39
Aug 10	7 8	19 23	Aug 14	8 20	19 38
Aug 20	7 19	19 22	Aug 24	8 31	19 38
Aug 30	7 29	19 21	Sep 3	8 40	19 37
Sep 9	7 36	19 21	Sep 13	8 47	19 36
Sep 19	7 42	19 20	Sep 23	8 52	19 36
Sep 29	7 46	19 20	Oct 3	8 55	19 35
Oct 9	7 47R	19 19	Oct 13	8 55R	19 35
Oct 19	7 46	19 19	Oct 23	8 53	19 35
Oct 29	7 42	19 19	Nov 2	8 49	19 35
Nov 8	7 37	19 19	Nov 12	8 42	19 35
Nov 18	7 29	19 19	Nov 22	8 34	19 36
Nov 28	7 20	19 20	Dec 2	8 24	19 37
Dec 8	7 9	19 20	Dec 12	8 13	19 37
Dec 18	6 58	19 21	Dec 22	8 2	19 38
Dec 28	6 46	19 22	Jan 1	7 49	19 40

1921		LONG	DEC	1922		LONG	DEC
		CANCER	NORTH			CANCER	NORTH
Jan	1	7 49R	19 40	Jan	6	8 53R	19 57
Jan	11	7 37	19 41	Jan	16	8 41	19 58
Jan	21	7 25	19 42	Jan	26	8 30	20 0
Jan	31	7 15	19 44	Feb	5	8 20	20 1
Feb	10	7 5	19 46	Feb	15	8 11	20 3
Feb	20	6 58	19 47	Feb	25	8 4	20 5
Mar	2	6 52	19 49	Mar	7	7 59	20 6
Mar	12	6 49	19 50	Mar	17	7 57	20 7
Mar	22	6 48D	19 51	Mar	27	7 57D	20 9
Apr	1	6 49	19 53	Apr	6	7 59	20 10
Apr	11	6 53	19 54	Apr	16	8 3	20 11
Apr	21	6 59	19 55	Apr	26	8 10	20 12
May	1	7 7	19 56	May	6	8 19	20 12
May	11	7 17	19 56	May	16	8 29	20 13
May	21	7 28	19 57	May	26	8 41	20 13
May	31	7 41	19 57	Jun	5	8 54	20 13
Jun	10	7 55	19 57	Jun	15	9 9	20 13
Jun	20	8 9	19 57	Jun	25	9 23	20 13
Jun	30	8 24	19 57	Jul	5	9 38	20 12
Jul	10	8 39	19 56	Jul	15	9 53	20 11
Jul	20	8 54	19 56	Jul	25	10 8	20 11
Jul	30	9 8	19 55	Aug	4	10 22	20 10
Aug	9	9 21	19 54	Aug	14	10 34	20 9
Aug	19	9 33	19 54	Aug	24	10 46	20 9
Aug	29	9 43	19 53	Sep	3	10 55	20 8
Sep	8	9 51	19 52	Sep	13	11 3	20 7
Sep	18	9 58	19 52	Sep	23	11 9	20 7
Sep	28	10 2	19 51	Oct	3	11 12	20 6
Oct	8	10 4	19 51	Oct	13	11 13R	20 6
Oct	18	10 3R	19 51	Oct	23	11 12	20 6
Oct	28	10 1	19 51	Nov	2	11 8	20 6
Nov	7	9 56	19 51	Nov	12	11 3	20 7
Nov	17	9 48	19 52	Nov	22	10 55	20 8
Nov	27	9 40	19 52	Dec	2	10 45	20 8
Dec	7	9 29	19 53	Dec	12	10 34	20 10
Dec	17	9 18	19 54	Dec	22	10 23	20 11
Dec	27	9 6	19 55	Jan	1	10 10	20 12

1923	LONG	DEC	1924	LONG	DEC
	CANCER	NORTH		CANCER	NORTH
Jan 1	10 10R	20 12	Jan 6	11 15	20 29
Jan 11	9 58	20 14	Jan 16	11 3	20 30
Jan 21	9 46	20 15	Jan 26	10 51	20 32
Jan 31	9 35	20 17	Feb 5	10 41	20 34
Feb 10	9 25	20 19	Feb 15	10 31	20 35
Feb 20	9 17	20 20	Feb 25	10 24	20 37
Mar 2	9 11	20 22	Mar 6	10 19	20 38
Mar 12	9 7	20 23	Mar 16	10 15	20 40
Mar 22	9 5	20 24	Mar 26	10 14D	20 41
Apr 1	9 6D	20 26	Apr 5	10 16	20 42
Apr 11	9 9	20 27	Apr 15	10 20	20 43
Apr 21	9 14	20 27	Apr 25	10 26	20 44
May 1	9 22	20 28	May 5	10 34	20 44
May 11	9 31	20 28	May 15	10 44	20 44
May 21	9 42	20 29	May 25	10 56	20 44
May 31	9 55	20 29	Jun 4	11 9	20 44
Jun 10	10 8	20 28	Jun 14	11 23	20 43
Jun 20	10 23	20 28	Jun 24	11 38	20 43
Jun 30	10 38	20 28	Jul 4	11 53	20 42
Jul 10	10 53	20 27	Jul 14	12 8	20 41
Jul 20	11 8	20 26	Jul 24	12 23	20 41
Jul 30	11 22	20 25	Aug 3	12 37	20 40
Aug 9	11 36	20 25	Aug 13	12 51	20 39
Aug 19	11 48	20 24	Aug 23	13 2	20 38
Aug 29	11 59	20 23	Sep 2	13 13	20 37
Sep 8	12 8	20 22	Sep 12	13 21	20 36
Sep 18	12 15	20 22	Sep 22	13 28	20 36
Sep 28	12 20	20 21	Oct 2	13 32	20 36
Oct 8	12 23	20 21	Oct 12	13 33	20 35
Oct 18	12 23R	20 21	Oct 22	13 33R	20 35
Oct 28	12 21	20 21	Nov 1	13 30	20 36
Nov 7	12 16	20 22	Nov 11	13 25	20 37
Nov 17	12 10	20 22	Nov 21	13 17	20 37
Nov 27	12 1	20 23	Dec 1	13 8	20 39
Dec 7	11 51	20 24	Dec 11	12 58	20 40
Dec 17	11 40	20 26	Dec 21	12 46	20 41
Dec 27	11 28	20 27	Dec 31	12 34	20 43

1925	LONG	DEC	1926	LONG	LAT
	CANCER	NORTH		CANCER	NORTH
Jan 10	12 21R	20 45	Jan 5	13 40R	20 59
Jan 20	12 9	20 47	Jan 15	13 27	21 1
Jan 30	11 57	20 48	Jan 25	13 16	21 2
Feb 9	11 47	20 50	Feb 4	13 4	21 4
Feb 19	11 38	20 52	Feb 14	12 55	21 6
Mar 1	11 32	20 53	Feb 24	12 47	21 8
Mar 11	11 27	20 55	Mar 6	12 41	21 9
Mar 21	11 25	20 56	Mar 16	12 37	21 11
Mar 31	11 25D	20 57	Mar 26	12 35	21 12
Apr 10	11 27	20 58	Apr 5	12 36D	21 13
Apr 20	11 32	20 59	Apr 15	12 39	21 13
Apr 30	11 39	20 59	Apr 25	12 45	21 14
May 10	11 48	20 59	May 5	12 53	21 14
May 20	11 59	20 59	May 15	13 2	21 14
May 30	12 11	20 59	May 25	13 14	21 14
Jun 9	12 24	20 58	Jun 4	13 27	21 13
Jun 19	12 39	20 58	Jun 14	13 41	21 13
Jun 29	12 54	20 57	Jun 24	13 55	21 12
Jul 9	13 9	20 56	Jul 4	14 11	21 11
Jul 19	13 24	20 55	Jul 14	14 26	21 10
Jul 29	13 39	20 54	Jul 24	14 41	21 9
Aug 8	13 53	20 53	Aug 3	14 56	21 8
Aug 18	14 6	20 52	Aug 13	15 9	21 6
Aug 28	14 17	20 51	Aug 23	15 22	21 6
Sep 7	14 27	20 51	Sep 2	15 33	21 5
Sep 17	14 35	20 50	Sep 12	15 42	21 4
Sep 27	14 40	20 50	Sep 22	15 49	21 3
Oct 7	14 44	20 50	Oct 2	15 54	21 3
Oct 17	14 45R	20 49	Oct 12	15 56	21 3
Oct 27	14 43	20 50	Oct 22	15 56R	21 3
Nov 6	14 39	20 51	Nov 1	15 54	21 4
Nov 16	14 33	20 51	Nov 11	15 49	21 4
Nov 26	14 25	20 52	Nov 21	15 43	21 6
Dec 6	14 16	20 54	Dec 1	15 34	21 7
Dec 16	14 5	20 55	Dec 11	15 24	21 8
Dec 26	13 53	20 57	Dec 21	15 12	21 10
Jan 5	13 40	20 59	Dec 31	15 0	21 12

1927	LONG	DEC	1928	LONG	DEC
	CANCER	NORTH		CANCER	NORTH
Jan 10	14 47R	21 14	Jan 5	16 8R	21 27
Jan 20	14 35	21 16	Jan 15	15 55	21 29
Jan 30	14 23	21 18	Jan 25	15 43	21 31
Feb 9	14 12	21 20	Feb 4	15 31	21 33
Feb 19	14 3	21 22	Feb 14	15 21	21 35
Mar 1	13 56	21 23	Feb 24	15 13	21 37
Mar 11	13 50	21 25	Mar 5	15 6	21 39
Mar 21	13 47	21 26	Mar 15	15 1	21 40
Mar 31	13 47D	21 27	Mar 25	14 59	21 41
Apr 10	13 48	21 28	Apr 4	14 59D	21 42
Apr 20	13 53	21 28	Apr 14	15 2	21 42
Apr 30	13 59	21 28	Apr 24	15 7	21 42
May 10	14 7	21 28	May 4	15 14	21 42
May 20	14 18	21 28	May 14	15 24	21 42
May 30	14 30	21 27	May 24	15 35	21 41
Jun 9	14 43	21 27	Jun 3	15 47	21 41
Jun 19	14 58	21 26	Jun 13	16 1	21 40
Jun 29	15 13	21 25	Jun 23	16 16	21 39
Jul 9	15 28	21 24	Jul 3	16 31	21 38
Jul 19	15 44	21 23	Jul 13	16 47	21 36
Jul 29	15 59	21 21	Jul 23	17 2	21 35
Aug 8	16 13	21 20	Aug 2	17 17	21 34
Aug 18	16 26	21 19	Aug 12	17 31	21 32
Aug 28	16 38	21 18	Aug 22	17 44	21 31
Sep 7	16 49	21 17	Sep 1	17 56	21 30
Sep 17	16 57	21 17	Sep 11	18 6	21 30
Sep 27	17 4	21 16	Sep 21	18 13	21 29
Oct 7	17 18	21 16	Oct 1	18 19	21 28
Oct 17	17 9	21 16	Oct 11	18 22	21 29
Oct 27	17 9R	21 17	Oct 21	18 23R	21 29
Nov 6	17 6	21 17	Oct 31	18 22	21 29
Nov 16	17 0	21 18	Nov 10	18 18	21 31
Nov 26	16 53	21 20	Nov 20	18 11	21 32
Dec 6	16 43	21 21	Nov 30	18 3	21 33
Dec 16	16 32	21 23	Dec 10	17 53	21 35
Dec 26	16 20	21 25	Dec 20	17 42	21 37
Jan 5	16 8	21 27	Dec 30	17 30	21 39

1929	LONG	DEC	1930	LONG	DEC
	CANCER	NORTH		CANCER	NORTH
Jan 9	17 17R	21 42	Jan 4	18 40R	21 53
Jan 19	17 4	21 44	Jan 14	18 27	21 56
Jan 29	16 52	21 46	Jan 24	18 14	21 58
Feb 8	16 41	21 48	Feb 3	18 2	22 0
Feb 18	16 31	21 50	Feb 13	17 52	22 2
Feb 28	16 23	21 52	Feb 23	17 42	22 4
Mar 10	16 17	21 53	Mar 5	17 35	22 5
Mar 20	16 14	21 54	Mar 15	17 30	22 7
Mar 30	16 12D	21 55	Mar 25	17 27	22 8
Apr 9	16 13	21 55	Apr 4	17 27D	22 8
Apr 19	16 17	21 56	Apr 14	17 28	22 9
Apr 29	16 23	21 56	Apr 24	17 33	22 9
May 9	16 31	21 56	May 4	17 40	22 9
May 19	16 41	21 55	May 14	17 48	22 8
May 29	16 52	21 55	May 24	17 59	22 8
Jun 8	17 6	21 53	Jun 3	18 11	22 7
Jun 18	17 20	21 52	Jun 13	18 25	22 5
Jun 28	17 35	21 51	Jun 23	18 40	22 4
Jul 8	17 50	21 50	Jul 3	18 55	22 3
Jul 18	18 6	21 48	Jul 13	19 11	22 1
Jul 28	18 22	21 47	Jul 23	19 26	21 59
Aug 7	18 36	21 45	Aug 2	19 42	21 58
Aug 17	18 50	21 44	Aug 12	19 57	21 56
Aug 27	19 3	21 43	Aug 22	20 10	21 55
Sep 6	19 14	21 42	Sep 1	20 22	21 54
Sep 16	19 23	21 41	Sep 11	20 33	21 53
Sep 26	19 30	21 40	Sep 21	20 41	21 52
Oct 6	19 35	21 41	Oct 1	20 48	21 52
Oct 16	19 38	21 41	Oct 11	20 52	21 52
Oct 26	19 38R	21 41	Oct 21	20 53	21 52
Nov 5	19 35	21 42	Oct 31	20 53R	21 53
Nov 15	19 30	21 43	Nov 10	20 49	21 54
Nov 25	19 23	21 45	Nov 20	20 44	21 55
Dec 5	19 14	21 47	Nov 30	20 36	21 58
Dec 15	19 4	21 49	Dec 10	20 26	22 0
Dec 25	18 52	21 51	Dec 20	20 15	22 2
Jan 4	18 40	21 53	Dec 30	20 3	22 4

1931	LONG	DEC	1932	LONG	DEC
	CANCER	NORTH		CANCER	NORTH
Jan 9	19 51R	22 7	Jan 4	21 15R	22 17
Jan 19	19 38	22 9	Jan 14	21 2	22 20
Jan 29	19 25	22 11	Jan 24	20 50	22 22
Feb 3	19 14	22 14	Feb 3	20 37	22 24
Feb 18	19 3	22 16	Feb 13	20 26	22 27
Feb 28	18 55	22 17	Feb 23	20 16	22 29
Mar 10	18 48	22 19	Mar 4	20 8	22 30
Mar 20	18 44	22 20	Mar 14	20 2	22 32
Mar 30	18 42	22 21	Mar 24	19 59	22 33
Apr 9	18 42D	22 21	Apr 3	19 57D	22 33
Apr 19	18 45	22 22	Apr 13	19 59	22 34
Apr 29	18 50	22 21	Apr 23	20 2	22 34
May 9	18 58	22 21	May 3	20 8	22 33
May 19	19 7	22 20	May 13	20 17	22 33
May 29	19 18	22 19	May 23	20 27	22 31
Jun 8	19 31	22 18	Jun 2	20 39	22 30
Jun 18	19 45	22 17	Jun 12	20 52	22 29
Jun 28	20 1	22 15	Jun 22	21 7	22 27
Jul 8	20 16	22 13	Jul 2	21 22	22 25
Jul 18	20 32	22 12	Jul 12	21 38	22 23
Jul 28	20 48	22 10	Jul 22	21 54	22 22
Aug 7	21 3	22 8	Aug 1	22 10	22 20
Aug 17	21 17	22 7	Aug 11	22 25	22 18
Aug 27	21 31	22 5	Aug 21	22 39	22 16
Sep 6	21 42	22 4	Aug 31	22 52	22 15
Sep 16	21 52	22 3	Sep 10	23 3	22 14
Sep 26	22 0	22 3	Sep 20	23 13	22 13
Oct 6	22 6	22 3	Sep 30	23 20	22 13
Oct 16	22 9	22 3	Oct 10	23 25	22 13
Oct 26	22 10R	22 4	Oct 20	23 27	22 13
Nov 5	22 8	22 5	Oct 30	23 27R	22 14
Nov 15	22 4	22 6	Nov 9	23 24	22 15
Nov 25	21 58	22 8	Nov 19	23 20	22 17
Dec 5	21 49	22 10	Nov 29	23 12	22 19
Dec 15	21 39	22 12	Dec 9	23 3	22 21
Dec 25	21 28	22 14	Dec 19	22 53	22 24
Jan 4	21 15	22 17	Dec 29	22 41	22 27

1933	LONG	DEC	1934	LONG	DEC
	CANCER	NORTH		CANCER	NORTH
Jan 8	22 28R	22 29	Jan 3	23 54R	22 38
Jan 18	22 15	22 32	Jan 13	23 41	22 41
Jan 28	22 2	22 35	Jan 23	23 28	22 44
Feb 7	21 50	22 37	Feb 2	23 16	22 47
Feb 17	21 39	22 39	Feb 12	23 4	22 49
Feb 27	21 30	22 41	Feb 22	22 54	22 51
Mar 9	21 23	22 43	Mar 4	22 45	22 53
Mar 19	21 17	22 44	Mar 14	22 38	22 54
Mar 29	21 15	22 45	Mar 24	22 34	22 55
Apr 8	21 14D	22 46	Apr 3	22 32	22 56
Apr 18	21 17	22 45	Apr 13	22 32D	22 56
Apr 28	21 21	22 45	Apr 23	22 35	22 56
May 8	21 28	22 45	May 3	22 41	22 56
May 18	21 37	22 43	May 13	22 49	22 54
May 28	21 48	22 42	May 23	22 58	22 53
Jun 7	22 1	22 41	Jun 2	23 10	22 52
Jun 17	22 15	22 39	Jun 12	23 23	22 50
Jun 27	22 30	22 37	Jun 22	23 38	22 48
Jul 7	22 45	22 35	Jul 2	23 53	22 46
Jul 17	23 1	22 33	Jul 12	24 9	22 44
Jul 27	23 17	22 31	Jul 22	24 25	22 41
Aug 6	23 33	22 29	Aug 1	24 41	22 39
Aug 16	23 48	22 27	Aug 11	24 57	22 37
Aug 26	24 2	22 25	Aug 21	25 12	22 35
Sep 5	24 14	22 24	Aug 31	25 25	22 34
Sep 15	24 25	22 23	Sep 10	25 37	22 33
Sep 25	24 33	22 23	Sep 20	25 47	22 32
Oct 5	24 40	22 22	Sep 30	25 55	22 31
Oct 15	24 44	22 23	Oct 10	26 1	22 31
Oct 25	24 46	22 23	Oct 20	26 4	22 32
Nov 4	24 45R	22 24	Oct 30	26 5R	22 32
Nov 14	24 41	22 26	Nov 9	26 3	22 34
Nov 24	24 36	22 28	Nov 19	25 59	22 36
Dec 4	24 28	22 30	Nov 29	25 52	22 38
Dec 14	24 18	22 33	Dec 9	25 43	22 40
Dec 24	24 7	22 35	Dec 19	25 33	22 43
Jan 3	23 54	22 38	Dec 29	25 21	22 46

1935		LONG	DEC	1936		LONG	DEC
		CANCER	NORTH			CANCER	NORTH
Jan	8	25 9R	22 49	Jan	3	26 37R	22 56
Jan	18	24 56	22 52	Jan	13	26 24	23 0
Jan	28	24 42	22 55	Jan	23	26 11	23 3
Feb	7	24 30	22 58	Feb	2	25 58	23 6
Feb	17	24 19	23 0	Feb	12	25 46	23 8
Feb	27	24 9	23 3	Feb	22	25 35	23 11
Mar	9	24 1	23 4	Mar	3	25 25	23 13
Mar	19	23 55	23 5	Mar	13	25 18	23 14
Mar	29	23 51	23 6	Mar	23	25 13	23 16
Apr	8	23 50D	23 6	Apr	2	25 10	23 16
Apr	18	23 52	23 6	Apr	12	25 10D	23 16
Apr	28	23 55	23 6	Apr	22	25 12	23 16
May	8	24 2	23 5	May	2	25 17	23 15
May	18	24 10	23 4	May	12	25 24	23 14
May	28	24 21	23 3	May	22	25 33	23 13
Jun	7	24 33	23 0	Jun	1	25 44	23 11
Jun	17	24 47	22 58	Jun	11	25 57	23 8
Jun	27	25 2	22 56	Jun	21	26 12	23 6
Jul	7	25 18	22 54	Jul	1	26 27	23 4
Jul	17	25 34	22 51	Jul	11	26 43	23 1
Jul	27	25 50	22 49	Jul	21	26 59	22 59
Aug	6	26 6	22 47	Jul	31	27 16	22 56
Aug	16	26 21	22 45	Aug	10	27 32	22 54
Aug	26	26 36	22 43	Aug	20	27 47	22 51
Sep	5	26 49	22 42	Aug	30	28 1	22 50
Sep	15	27 0	22 40	Sep	9	28 14	22 48
Sep	25	27 10	22 39	Sep	19	28 25	22 47
Oct	5	27 17	22 39	Sep	29	28 33	22 47
Oct	15	27 22	22 40	Oct	9	28 40	22 47
Oct	25	27 25	22 40	Oct	19	28 44	22 47
Nov	4	27 24R	22 41	Oct	29	28 46	22 48
Nov	14	27 22	22 43	Nov	8	28 45R	22 50
Nov	24	27 17	22 45	Nov	18	28 41	22 51
Dec	4	27 9	22 48	Nov	28	28 35	22 54
Dec	14	27 0	22 50	Dec	8	28 27	22 57
Dec	24	26 49	22 53	Dec	18	28 17	22 59
Jan	3	26 37	22 56	Dec	28	28 6	23 3

1937	LONG	DEC	1938	LONG	DEC
	CANCER	NORTH		CANCER	NORTH
Jan 7	27 53R	23 6	Jan 2	29 23R	23 12
Jan 17	27 40	23 10	Jan 12	29 10	23 15
Jan 27	27 27	23 13	Jan 22	28 57	23 19
Feb 6	27 14	23 16	Feb 1	28 44	23 22
Feb 16	27 2	23 19	Feb 11	28 31	23 25
Feb 26	26 52	23 21	Feb 21	28 20	23 27
Mar 8	26 43	23 22	Mar 3	28 10	23 30
Mar 18	26 36	23 24	Mar 13	28 1	23 32
Mar 28	26 32	23 25	Mar 23	27 56	23 32
Apr 7	26 30	23 25	Apr 2	27 52	23 33
Apr 17	26 30D	23 25	Apr 12	27 51D	23 34
Apr 27	26 34	23 24	Apr 22	27 53	23 33
May 7	26 39	23 23	May 2	27 57	23 32
May 17	26 47	23 22	May 12	28 3	23 31
May 27	26 57	23 20	May 22	28 12	23 29
Jun 6	27 9	23 18	Jun 1	28 23	23 27
Jun 16	27 23	23 16	Jun 11	28 35	23 25
Jun 26	27 38	23 13	Jun 21	28 49	23 22
Jul 6	27 53	23 10	Jul 1	29 5	23 19
Jul 16	28 10	23 8	Jul 11	29 21	23 16
Jul 26	28 26	23 5	Jul 21	29 37	23 13
Aug 5	28 42	23 2	Jul 31	29 54	23 10
Aug 15	28 58	23 0		LEO	
Aug 25	29 13	22 58	Aug 10	0 10	23 7
Sep 4	29 27	22 56	Aug 20	0 26	23 5
Sep 14	29 39	22 54	Aug 30	0 41	23 3
Sep 24	29 50	22 54	Sep 9	0 54	23 1
Oct 4	29 58	22 53	Sep 19	1 6	23 0
	LEO		Sep 29	1 15	22 59
Oct 14	0 4	22 53	Oct 9	1 23	22 59
Oct 24	0 7	22 54	Oct 19	1 28	22 59
Nov 3	0 8R	22 55	Oct 29	1 30	23 0
Nov 13	0 6	22 57	Nov 8	1 30R	23 1
Nov 23	0 1	22 59	Nov 18	1 28	23 4
	CANCER		Nov 28	1 22	23 6
Dec 3	29 55	23 2	Dec 8	1 15	23 9
Dec 13	29 46	23 5	Dec 18	1 5	23 13
Dec 23	29 35	23 8	Dec 28	0 54	23 16
Jan 2	29 23	23 12			

1939	LONG	DEC	1940	LONG	DEC
	LEO	NORTH		LEO	NORTH
Jan 7	0 42R	23 20	Jan 2	2 14R	23 23
Jan 17	0 29	23 23	Jan 12	2 1	23 27
Jan 27	0 15	23 37	Jan 22	1 48	23 31
Feb 6	0 2	23 31	Feb 1	1 34	23 35
	CANCER		Feb 11	1 22	23 38
Feb 16	29 50	23 33	Feb 21	1 9	23 41
Feb 26	29 39	23 36	Mar 2	0 59	23 44
Mar 8	29 29	23 38	Mar 12	0 50	23 45
Mar 18	29 22	23 39	Mar 22	0 43	23 46
Mar 28	29 16	23 40	Apr 1	0 39	23 48
Apr 7	29 14	23 41	Apr 11	0 37	23 47
Apr 17	29 14D	23 40	Apr 21	0 38D	23 47
Apr 27	29 16	23 40	May 1	0 41	23 46
May 7	29 21	23 39	May 11	0 47	23 44
May 17	29 28	23 37	May 21	0 55	23 42
May 27	29 38	23 35	May 31	1 5	23 40
Jun 6	29 49	23 33	Jun 10	1 17	23 37
	LEO		Jun 20	1 31	23 34
Jun 16	0 3	23 30	Jun 30	1 46	23 31
Jun 26	0 17	23 27	Jul 10	2 3	23 28
Jul 6	0 33	23 24	Jul 20	2 19	23 24
Jul 16	0 49	23 21	Jul 30	2 36	23 21
Jul 26	1 6	23 18	Aug 9	2 53	23 18
Aug 5	1 23	23 14	Aug 19	3 9	23 15
Aug 15	1 39	23 12	Aug 29	3 24	23 12
Aug 25	1 55	23 9	Sep 8	3 39	23 11
Sep 4	2 9	23 7	Sep 18	3 51	23 9
Sep 14	2 22	23 6	Sep 28	4 2	23 8
Sep 24	2 33	23 5	Oct 8	4 10	23 8
Oct 4	2 42	23 3	Oct 18	4 16	23 8
Oct 14	2 49	23 4	Oct 28	4 20	23 8
Oct 24	2 53	23 5	Nov 7	4 20R	23 11
Nov 3	2 55	23 5	Nov 17	4 19	23 13
Nov 13	2 54R	23 8	Nov 27	4 14	23 15
Nov 23	2 50	23 10	Dec 7	4 7	23 18
Dec 3	2 44	23 12	Dec 17	3 58	23 22
Dec 13	2 36	23 16	Dec 27	3 47	23 26
Dec 23	2 26	23 20			
Jan 2	2 14	23 23			

1941	LONG	DEC	1942	LONG	DEC
	LEO	NORTH		LEO	NORTH
Jan 6	3 35R	23 30	Jan 1	5 10R	23 31
Jan 16	3 22	23 34	Jan 11	4 58	23 35
Jan 26	3 9	23 38	Jan 21	4 44	23 40
Feb 5	2 55	23 41	Jan 31	4 31	23 43
Feb 15	2 42	23 44	Feb 10	4 17	23 47
Feb 25	2 31	23 48	Feb 20	4 5	23 51
Mar 7	2 21	23 49	Mar 2	3 53	23 53
Mar 17	2 12	23 51	Mar 12	3 44	23 55
Mar 27	2 6	23 53	Mar 22	3 36	23 57
Apr 6	2 3	23 53	Apr 1	3 31	23 57
Apr 16	2 2D	23 53	Apr 11	3 28	23 57
Apr 26	2 3	23 52	Apr 21	3 28D	23 58
May 6	2 8	23 50	May 1	3 31	23 56
May 16	2 14	23 49	May 11	3 36	23 54
May 26	2 23	23 47	May 21	3 43	23 52
Jun 5	2 34	23 44	May 31	3 53	23 49
Jun 15	2 47	23 40	Jun 10	4 5	23 46
Jun 25	3 2	23 37	Jun 20	4 18	23 43
Jul 5	3 17	23 34	Jun 30	4 33	23 39
Jul 15	3 34	23 30	Jul 10	4 49	23 36
Jul 25	3 51	23 27	Jul 20	5 6	23 32
Aug 4	4 8	23 24	Jul 30	5 23	23 28
Aug 14	4 24	23 20	Aug 9	5 41	23 25
Aug 24	4 41	23 17	Aug 19	5 57	23 21
Sep 3	4 56	23 15	Aug 29	6 13	23 19
Sep 13	5 9	23 13	Sep 8	6 28	23 17
Sep 23	5 21	23 11	Sep 18	6 41	23 14
Oct 3	5 31	23 11	Sep 28	6 53	23 14
Oct 13	5 39	23 11	Oct 8	7 2	23 13
Oct 23	5 44	23 11	Oct 18	7 9	23 12
Nov 2	5 47	23 13	Oct 28	7 14	23 14
Nov 12	5 47R	23 14	Nov 7	7 15	23 15
Nov 22	5 44	23 16	Nov 17	7 15R	23 17
Dec 2	5 39	23 20	Nov 27	7 11	23 20
Dec 12	5 31	23 23	Dec 7	7 5	23 24
Dec 22	5 22	23 27	Dec 17	6 56	23 27
Jan 1	5 10	23 31	Dec 27	6 46	23 31

1943	LONG	DEC	1944	LONG	DEC
	LEO	NORTH		LEO	NORTH
Jan 6	6 34R	23 36	Jan 1	8 12R	23 35
Jan 16	6 21	23 40	Jan 11	7 59	23 39
Jan 26	6 8	23 44	Jan 21	7 46	23 44
Feb 5	5 54	23 48	Jan 31	7 32	23 48
Feb 15	5 41	23 52	Feb 10	7 19	23 52
Feb 25	5 28	23 55	Feb 20	7 6	23 55
Mar 7	5 18	23 57	Mar 1	6 54	23 58
Mar 17	5 9	24 0	Mar 11	6 43	24 1
Mar 27	5 2	24 0	Mar 21	6 35	24 2
Apr 6	4 57	24 1	Mar 31	6 29	24 3
Apr 16	4 55	24 2	Apr 10	6 25	24 4
Apr 26	4 56D	24 0	Apr 20	6 24D	24 3
May 6	5 0	23 59	Apr 30	6 26	24 2
May 16	5 6	23 57	May 10	6 30	24 1
May 26	5 14	23 54	May 20	6 37	23 58
Jun 5	5 25	23 51	May 30	6 46	23 55
Jun 15	5 37	23 48	Jun 9	6 58	23 52
Jun 25	5 51	23 44	Jun 19	7 11	23 48
Jul 5	6 7	23 40	Jun 29	7 25	23 44
Jul 15	6 23	23 36	Jul 9	7 41	23 40
Jul 25	6 40	23 33	Jul 19	7 58	23 36
Aug 4	6 58	23 29	Jul 29	8 16	23 32
Aug 14	7 15	23 25	Aug 8	8 33	23 28
Aug 24	7 32	23 22	Aug 18	8 50	23 24
Sep 3	7 47	23 19	Aug 28	9 7	23 21
Sep 13	8 2	23 16	Sep 7	9 22	23 18
Sep 23	8 15	23 15	Sep 17	9 37	23 16
Oct 3	8 26	23 14	Sep 27	9 49	23 15
Oct 13	8 34	23 13	Oct 7	9 59	23 13
Oct 23	8 41	23 14	Oct 17	10 7	23 14
Nov 2	8 44	23 15	Oct 27	10 13	23 14
Nov 12	8 45R	23 16	Nov 6	10 16	23 15
Nov 22	8 43	23 20	Nov 16	10 16R	23 18
Dec 2	8 39	23 23	Nov 26	10 13	23 21
Dec 12	8 32	23 26	Dec 6	10 8	23 24
Dec 22	8 23	23 30	Dec 16	10 0	23 28
Jan 1	8 12	23 35	Dec 26	9 50	23 33

1945	LONG	DEC	1946	LONG	DEC
	LEO	NORTH		LEO	NORTH
Jan 5	9 39R	23 37	Jan 10	11 7R	23 38
Jan 15	9 26	23 42	Jan 20	10 54	23 43
Jan 25	9 12	23 46	Jan 30	10 40	23 48
Feb 4	8 58	23 51	Feb 9	10 26	23 52
Feb 14	8 45	23 55	Feb 19	10 12	23 56
Feb 24	8 32	23 58	Mar 1	10 0	24 0
Mar 6	8 20	24 2	Mar 11	9 49	24 2
Mar 16	8 11	24 3	Mar 21	9 40	24 4
Mar 26	8 3	24 5	Mar 31	9 33	24 6
Apr 5	7 58	24 6	Apr 10	9 28	24 6
Apr 15	7 55	24 5	Apr 20	9 26	24 5
Apr 25	7 55D	24 4	Apr 30	9 27D	24 5
May 5	7 57	24 3	May 10	9 30	24 2
May 15	8 3	24 1	May 20	9 36	24 0
May 25	8 10	23 58	May 30	9 45	23 57
Jun 4	8 20	23 55	Jun 9	9 56	23 53
Jun 14	8 32	23 51	Jun 19	10 8	23 49
Jun 24	8 46	23 47	Jun 29	10 23	23 45
Jul 4	9 1	23 43	Jul 9	10 39	23 40
Jul 14	9 18	23 39	Jul 19	10 56	23 36
Jul 24	9 35	23 34	Jul 29	11 13	23 31
Aug 3	9 53	23 30	Aug 8	11 31	23 27
Aug 13	10 10	23 26	Aug 18	11 49	23 23
Aug 23	10 27	23 22	Aug 28	12 6	23 19
Sep 2	10 44	23 19	Sep 7	12 22	23 16
Sep 12	10 59	23 17	Sep 17	12 37	23 13
Sep 22	11 13	23 14	Sep 27	12 50	23 11
Oct 2	11 25	23 12	Oct 7	13 2	23 10
Oct 12	11 34	23 12	Oct 17	13 11	23 10
Oct 22	11 42	23 13	Oct 27	13 17	23 10
Nov 1	11 46	23 13	Nov 6	13 21	23 12
Nov 11	11 48	23 15	Nov 16	13 22R	23 14
Nov 21	11 48R	23 18	Nov 26	13 20	23 16
Dec 1	11 44	23 20	Dec 6	13 16	23 20
Dec 11	11 38	23 25	Dec 16	13 9	23 24
Dec 21	11 29	23 29	Dec 26	13 0	23 29
Dec 31	11 19	23 33	Jan 5	12 49	23 34

1947	LONG	DEC	1948	LONG	DEC
	LEO	NORTH		LEO	NORTH
Jan 5	12 49R	23 34	Jan 10	14 20R	23 33
Jan 15	12 36	23 39	Jan 20	14 7	23 38
Jan 25	12 23	23 44	Jan 30	13 53	23 43
Feb 4	12 9	23 48	Feb 9	13 39	23 48
Feb 14	11 55	23 53	Feb 19	13 25	23 53
Feb 24	11 41	23 57	Feb 29	13 12	23 56
Mar 6	11 29	24 0	Mar 10	13 0	23 59
Mar 16	11 19	24 2	Mar 20	12 50	24 2
Mar 26	11 10	24 5	Mar 30	12 42	24 3
Apr 5	11 4	24 5	Apr 9	12 37	24 3
Apr 15	11 0	24 5	Apr 19	12 34	24 4
Apr 25	10 59D	24 5	Apr 29	12 33D	24 2
May 5	11 1	24 3	May 9	12 36	24 0
May 15	11 5	24 0	May 19	12 41	23 58
May 25	11 12	23 58	May 29	12 49	23 54
Jun 4	11 21	23 54	Jun 8	12 59	23 50
Jun 14	11 33	23 50	Jun 18	13 11	23 46
Jun 24	11 46	23 46	Jun 28	13 26	23 41
Jul 4	12 1	23 41	Jul 8	13 41	23 36
Jul 14	12 18	23 36	Jul 18	13 58	23 31
Jul 24	12 35	23 32	Jul 28	14 16	23 26
Aug 3	12 53	23 27	Aug 7	14 34	23 22
Aug 13	13 11	23 23	Aug 17	14 52	23 17
Aug 23	13 28	23 18	Aug 27	15 10	23 13
Sep 2	13 45	23 15	Sep 6	15 26	23 9
Sep 12	14 1	23 13	Sep 16	15 42	23 6
Sep 22	14 16	23 9	Sep 26	15 56	23 4
Oct 2	14 29	23 8	Oct 6	16 9	23 2
Oct 12	14 40	23 7	Oct 16	16 19	23 1
Oct 22	14 48	23 6	Oct 26	16 27	23 2
Nov 1	14 54	23 7	Nov 5	16 32	23 3
Nov 11	14 57	23 9	Nov 15	16 34	23 4
Nov 21	14 57R	23 11	Nov 25	16 33R	23 8
Dec 1	14 55	23 15	Dec 5	16 30	23 12
Dec 11	14 49	23 19	Dec 15	16 24	23 15
Dec 21	14 41	23 23	Dec 25	16 15	23 20
Dec 31	14 32	23 28	Jan 4	16 4	23 26

1949	LONG	DEC	1950	LONG	DEC
	LEO	NORTH		LEO	NORTH
Jan 4	16 4R	23 26	Jan 9	17 39R	23 22
Jan 14	15 52	23 31	Jan 19	17 26	23 28
Jan 24	15 39	23 36	Jan 29	17 12	23 33
Feb 3	15 25	23 41	Feb 8	16 58	23 39
Feb 13	15 10	23 47	Feb 18	16 44	23 43
Feb 23	14 57	23 50	Feb 28	16 30	23 47
Mar 5	14 44	23 54	Mar 10	16 17	23 52
Mar 15	14 32	23 58	Mar 20	16 7	23 53
Mar 25	14 23	23 59	Mar 30	15 58	23 55
Apr 4	14 16	24 0	Apr 9	15 51	23 57
Apr 14	14 11	24 1	Apr 19	15 47	23 56
Apr 24	14 9	24 0	Apr 29	15 46D	23 55
May 4	14 10D	23 58	May 9	15 48	23 54
May 14	14 13	23 56	May 19	15 52	23 50
May 24	14 19	23 53	May 29	15 59	23 47
Jun 3	14 28	23 49	Jun 8	16 8	23 43
Jun 13	14 39	23 45	Jun 18	16 20	23 38
Jun 23	14 52	23 40	Jun 28	16 34	23 33
Jul 3	15 7	23 35	Jul 8	16 49	23 28
Jul 13	15 23	23 30	Jul 18	17 6	23 22
Jul 23	15 40	23 25	Jul 28	17 24	23 17
Aug 2	15 58	23 20	Aug 7	17 42	23 11
Aug 12	16 16	23 14	Aug 17	18 0	23 7
Aug 22	16 34	23 10	Aug 27	18 19	23 2
Sep 1	16 52	23 6	Sep 6	18 36	22 57
Sep 11	17 9	23 2	Sep 16	18 53	22 54
Sep 21	17 24	23 0	Sep 26	19 8	22 51
Oct 1	17 38	22 57	Oct 6	19 21	22 49
Oct 11	17 50	22 55	Oct 16	19 33	22 48
Oct 21	18 0	22 56	Oct 26	19 41	22 48
Oct 31	18 6	22 56	Nov 5	19 48	22 48
Nov 10	18 11	22 57	Nov 15	19 51	22 51
Nov 20	18 12R	23 0	Nov 25	19 51R	22 54
Nov 30	18 10	23 3	Dec 5	19 49	22 57
Dec 10	18 6	23 7	Dec 15	19 44	23 2
Dec 20	17 59	23 12	Dec 25	19 36	23 7
Dec 30	17 50	23 17	Jan 4	19 26	23 12

1951	LONG	DEC	1952	LONG	DEC
	LEO	NORTH		LEO	NORTH
Jan 4	19 26R	23 12	Jan 9	21 4R	23 6
Jan 14	19 14	23 18	Jan 19	20 52	23 12
Jan 24	19 1	23 23	Jan 29	20 38	23 18
Feb 3	18 47	23 29	Feb 8	20 24	23 23
Feb 13	18 33	23 34	Feb 18	20 9	23 28
Feb 23	18 18	23 39	Feb 28	19 55	23 34
Mar 5	18 5	23 44	Mar 9	19 42	23 37
Mar 15	17 53	23 46	Mar 19	19 30	23 40
Mar 25	17 43	23 48	Mar 29	19 20	23 43
Apr 4	17 34	23 51	Apr 8	19 13	23 43
Apr 14	17 29	23 50	Apr 18	19 8	23 43
Apr 24	17 26	23 50	Apr 28	19 6	23 43
May 4	17 25D	23 49	May 8	19 6D	23 40
May 14	17 28	23 46	May 18	19 10	23 37
May 24	17 33	23 43	May 28	19 16	23 35
Jun 3	17 41	23 39	Jun 7	19 24	23 30
Jun 13	17 51	23 34	Jun 17	19 35	23 25
Jun 23	18 3	23 29	Jun 27	19 49	23 20
Jul 3	18 18	23 24	Jul 7	20 4	23 14
Jul 13	18 34	23 19	Jul 17	20 20	23 8
Jul 23	18 51	23 13	Jul 27	20 38	23 2
Aug 2	19 9	23 7	Aug 6	20 56	22 56
Aug 12	19 28	23 2	Aug 16	21 15	22 51
Aug 22	19 46	22 57	Aug 26	21 34	22 45
Sep 1	20 5	22 52	Sep 5	21 52	22 41
Sep 11	20 22	22 48	Sep 15	22 10	22 37
Sep 21	20 38	22 45	Sep 25	22 26	22 33
Oct 1	20 53	22 41	Oct 5	22 40	22 31
Oct 11	21 6	22 40	Oct 15	22 52	22 30
Oct 21	21 17	22 40	Oct 25	23 2	22 28
Oct 31	21 25	22 39	Nov 4	23 10	22 30
Nov 10	21 30	22 41	Nov 14	23 14	22 31
Nov 20	21 33	22 43	Nov 24	23 16R	22 33
Nov 30	21 32R	22 45	Dec 4	23 15	22 37
Dec 10	21 29	22 50	Dec 14	23 11	22 42
Dec 20	21 23	22 55	Dec 24	23 4	22 46
Dec 30	21 15	23 0	Jan 3	22 55	22 52

1953	LONG	DEC	1954	LONG	DEC
	LEO	NORTH		LEO	NORTH
Jan 3	22 55R	22 52	Jan 8	24 36R	22 43
Jan 13	22 43	22 58	Jan 18	24 24	22 49
Jan 23	22 30	23 4	Jan 28	24 11	22 55
Feb 2	22 16	23 10	Feb 7	23 57	23 1
Feb 12	22 2	23 16	Feb 17	23 42	23 8
Feb 22	21 47	23 22	Feb 27	23 27	23 12
Mar 4	21 33	23 25	Mar 9	23 14	23 16
Mar 14	21 21	23 29	Mar 19	23 1	23 21
Mar 24	21 9	23 33	Mar 29	22 51	23 22
Apr 3	21 0	23 34	Apr 8	22 42	23 24
Apr 13	20 53	23 34	Apr 18	22 36	23 25
Apr 23	20 49	23 35	Apr 28	22 33	23 23
May 3	20 48D	23 33	May 8	22 32D	23 22
May 13	20 49	23 30	May 18	22 34	23 20
May 23	20 54	23 28	May 28	22 40	23 15
Jun 2	21 1	23 23	Jun 7	22 47	23 11
Jun 12	21 10	23 19	Jun 17	22 58	23 6
Jun 22	21 22	23 14	Jun 27	23 11	23 0
Jul 2	21 36	23 8	Jul 7	23 25	22 54
Jul 12	21 52	23 2	Jul 17	23 41	22 48
Jul 22	22 9	22 56	Jul 27	23 59	22 42
Aug 1	22 27	22 50	Aug 6	24 18	22 35
Aug 11	22 46	22 44	Aug 16	24 37	22 29
Aug 21	23 5	22 38	Aug 26	24 56	22 24
Aug 31	23 23	22 33	Sep 5	25 15	22 18
Sep 10	23 42	22 28	Sep 15	25 33	22 13
Sep 20	23 59	22 23	Sep 25	25 50	22 10
Sep 30	24 15	22 21	Oct 5	26 5	22 7
Oct 10	24 29	22 19	Oct 15	26 19	22 4
Oct 20	24 40	22 17	Oct 25	26 30	22 4
Oct 30	24 50	22 18	Nov 4	26 39	22 4
Nov 9	24 56	22 18	Nov 14	26 45	22 5
Nov 19	25 0	22 19	Nov 24	26 48	22 8
Nov 29	25 1R	22 23	Dec 4	26 48R	22 11
Dec 9	24 59	22 27	Dec 14	26 45	22 15
Dec 19	24 54	22 31	Dec 24	26 39	22 21
Dec 29	24 46	22 37	Jan 3	26 30	22 26

1955	LONG	DEC	1956	LONG	DEC
	LEO	NORTH		LEO	NORTH
Jan 3	26 30R	22 26	Jan 8	28 16R	22 14
Jan 13	26 20	22 32	Jan 18	28 5	22 20
Jan 23	26 7	22 39	Jan 28	27 52	22 27
Feb 2	25 53	22 45	Feb 7	27 37	22 34
Feb 12	25 39	22 52	Feb 17	27 23	22 39
Feb 22	25 24	22 57	Feb 27	27 8	22 45
Mar 4	25 9	23 2	Mar 8	26 53	22 51
Mar 14	24 56	23 7	Mar 18	26 40	22 54
Mar 24	24 44	23 9	Mar 28	26 29	22 56
Apr 3	24 34	23 11	Apr 7	26 19	22 59
Apr 13	24 26	23 13	Apr 17	26 12	22 59
Apr 23	24 21	23 12	Apr 27	26 8	22 58
May 3	24 18	23 11	May 7	26 6	22 58
May 13	24 19D	23 10	May 17	26 7D	22 54
May 23	24 22	23 6	May 27	26 11	22 51
Jun 2	24 28	23 2	Jun 6	26 18	22 47
Jun 12	24 36	22 57	Jun 16	26 28	22 41
Jun 22	24 48	22 51	Jun 26	26 40	22 35
Jul 2	25 1	22 45	Jul 6	26 54	22 29
Jul 12	25 16	22 39	Jul 16	27 10	22 22
Jul 22	25 33	22 33	Jul 26	27 27	22 15
Aug 1	25 51	22 26	Aug 5	27 46	22 8
Aug 11	26 10	22 19	Aug 15	28 5	22 2
Aug 21	26 30	22 13	Aug 25	28 25	21 56
Aug 31	26 49	22 8	Sep 4	28 44	21 49
Sep 10	27 8	22 2	Sep 14	29 3	21 45
Sep 20	27 26	21 58	Sep 24	29 21	21 40
Sep 30	27 43	21 54	Oct 4	29 37	21 36
Oct 10	27 58	21 50	Oct 14	29 52	21 34
Oct 20	28 11	21 50		VIRGO	
Oct 30	28 21	21 49	Oct 24	0 4	21 33
Nov 9	28 29	21 49	Nov 3	0 14	21 32
Nov 19	28 35	21 51	Nov 13	0 22	21 34
Nov 29	28 37	21 54	Nov 23	0 26	21 36
Dec 9	28 36R	21 57	Dec 3	0 27R	21 38
Dec 19	28 32	22 3	Dec 13	0 26	21 43
Dec 29	28 25	22 8	Dec 23	0 21	21 48
			Jan 2	0 13	21 53

1957		LONG	DEC	1958		LONG	DEC
		VIRGO	NORTH			VIRGO	NORTH
Jan	2	0 13R	21 53	Jan	7	2 3R	21 38
Jan	12	0 3	22 0	Jan	17	1 52	21 45
		LEO		Jan	27	1 40	21 51
Jan	22	29 51	22 7	Feb	6	1 26	21 58
Feb	1	29 38	22 13	Feb	16	1 11	22 5
Feb	11	29 23	22 20	Feb	26	0 56	22 11
Feb	21	29 8	22 26	Mar	8	0 41	22 16
Mar	3	28 53	22 32	Mar	18	0 27	22 20
Mar	13	28 39	22 36	Mar	28	0 15	22 25
Mar	23	28 27	22 40	Apr	7	0 4	22 26
Apr	2	28 15	22 43			LEO	
Apr	12	28 7	22 44	Apr	17	29 56	22 27
Apr	22	28 0	22 44	Apr	27	29 50	22 28
May	2	27 56	22 44	May	7	29 47	22 26
May	12	27 56D	22 41	May	17	29 47D	22 23
May	22	27 58	22 38	May	27	29 50	22 21
Jun	1	28 3	22 35	Jun	6	29 56	22 15
Jun	11	28 10	22 29			VIRGO	
Jun	21	28 21	22 23	Jun	16	0 5	22 10
Jul	1	28 33	22 17	Jun	26	0 16	22 4
Jul	11	28 48	22 10	Jul	6	0 30	21 57
Jul	21	29 5	22 3	Jul	16	0 45	21 50
Jul	31	29 23	21 56	Jul	26	1 2	21 43
Aug	10	29 42	21 50	Aug	5	1 21	21 36
		VIRGO		Aug	15	1 40	21 29
Aug	20	0 2	21 43	Aug	25	2 0	21 21
Aug	30	0 21	21 36	Sep	4	2 20	21 16
Sep	9	0 41	21 31	Sep	14	2 40	21 10
Sep	19	1 0	21 26	Sep	24	2 58	21 4
Sep	29	1 17	21 20	Oct	4	3 16	21 1
Oct	9	1 34	21 18	Oct	14	3 31	20 58
Oct	19	1 48	21 16	Oct	24	3 45	20 54
Oct	29	2 0	21 14	Nov	3	3 57	20 55
Nov	8	2 9	21 15	Nov	13	4 5	20 55
Nov	18	2 16	21 16	Nov	23	4 11	20 56
Nov	28	2 19	21 17	Dec	3	4 14	21 0
Dec	8	2 19R	21 22	Dec	13	4 13R	21 4
Dec	18	2 17	21 27	Dec	23	4 10	21 8
Dec	28	2 11	21 31	Jan	2	4 3	21 15

1959	LONG	DEC	1960	LONG	DEC
	VIRGO	NORTH		VIRGO	NORTH
Jan 2	4 3R	21 15	Jan 7	5 57R	20 56
Jan 12	3 54	21 21	Jan 17	5 47	21 2
Jan 22	3 43	21 28	Jan 27	5 35	21 9
Feb 1	3 30	21 35	Feb 6	5 22	21 16
Feb 11	3 16	21 42	Feb 16	5 7	21 24
Feb 21	3 0	21 49	Feb 26	4 52	21 30
Mar 3	2 45	21 54	Mar 7	4 37	21 35
Mar 13	2 31	21 59	Mar 17	4 22	21 41
Mar 23	2 17	22 4	Mar 27	4 9	21 44
Apr 2	2 5	22 6	Apr 6	3 57	21 47
Apr 12	1 55	22 8	Apr 16	3 47	21 50
Apr 22	1 47	22 10	Apr 26	3 41	21 49
May 2	1 42	22 8	May 6	3 37	21 48
May 12	1 40	22 7	May 16	3 35D	21 47
May 22	1 41D	22 5	May 26	3 37	21 42
Jun 1	1 45	22 0	Jun 5	3 42	21 38
Jun 11	1 52	21 55	Jun 15	3 49	21 33
Jun 21	2 1	21 50	Jun 25	4 0	21 26
Jul 1	2 13	21 43	Jul 5	4 12	21 19
Jul 11	2 27	21 35	Jul 15	4 27	21 12
Jul 21	2 44	21 28	Jul 25	4 44	21 5
Jul 31	3 1	21 21	Aug 4	5 3	20 57
Aug 10	3 20	21 13	Aug 14	5 22	20 49
Aug 20	3 40	21 6	Aug 24	5 42	20 42
Aug 30	4 0	20 59	Sep 3	6 3	20 35
Sep 9	4 20	20 53	Sep 13	6 23	20 28
Sep 19	4 40	20 46	Sep 23	6 42	20 23
Sep 29	4 59	20 42	Oct 3	7 1	20 18
Oct 9	5 16	20 38	Oct 13	7 18	20 13
Oct 19	5 31	20 34	Oct 23	7 33	20 12
Oct 29	5 44	20 34	Nov 2	7 45	20 11
Nov 8	5 55	20 34	Nov 12	7 55	20 9
Nov 18	6 3	20 33	Nov 22	8 3	20 12
Nov 28	6 8	20 36	Dec 2	8 7	20 14
Dec 8	6 10	20 40	Dec 12	8 8R	20 17
Dec 18	6 9R	20 43	Dec 22	8 6	20 23
Dec 28	6 4	20 49	Jan 1	8 1	20 29

Mean Solar	0 hr		1 hr		2 hr		3 hr		4 hr		5 hr		6 hr		7 hr		8 hr		9 hr		10 hr		11 hr	
min	m	s	m	s	m	s	m	s	m	s	m	s	m	s	m	s	m	s	m	s	m	s	m	s
0	0	0	0	10	0	20	0	30	0	39	0	49	0	59	1	9	1	19	1	29	1	39	1	48
1	0	0	0	10	0	20	0	30	0	40	0	49	0	59	1	9	1	19	1	29	1	39	1	49
2	0	0	0	10	0	20	0	30	0	40	0	50	1	0	1	9	1	19	1	29	1	39	1	49
3	0	1	0	10	0	20	0	30	0	40	0	50	1	0	1	10	1	19	1	29	1	39	1	49
4	0	1	0	11	0	20	0	30	0	40	0	50	1	0	1	10	1	20	1	29	1	39	1	49
5	0	1	0	11	0	21	0	30	0	40	0	50	1	0	1	10	1	20	1	30	1	39	1	49
6	0	1	0	11	0	21	0	31	0	40	0	50	1	0	1	10	1	20	1	30	1	40	1	49
7	0	1	0	11	0	21	0	31	0	41	0	50	1	0	1	10	1	20	1	30	1	40	1	50
8	0	1	0	11	0	21	0	31	0	41	0	51	1	1	1	10	1	20	1	30	1	40	1	50
9	0	2	0	11	0	21	0	31	0	41	0	51	1	1	1	11	1	20	1	30	1	40	1	50
10	0	2	0	12	0	21	0	31	0	41	0	51	1	1	1	11	1	21	1	30	1	40	1	50
11	0	2	0	12	0	22	0	31	0	41	0	51	1	1	1	11	1	21	1	31	1	40	1	50
12	0	2	0	12	0	22	0	32	0	41	0	51	1	1	1	11	1	21	1	31	1	41	1	50
13	0	2	0	12	0	22	0	32	0	42	0	51	1	1	1	11	1	21	1	31	1	41	1	51
14	0	2	0	12	0	22	0	32	0	42	0	52	1	1	1	11	1	21	1	31	1	41	1	51
15	0	3	0	12	0	22	0	32	0	42	0	52	1	2	1	12	1	21	1	31	1	41	1	51
16	0	3	0	13	0	22	0	32	0	42	0	52	1	2	1	12	1	22	1	31	1	41	1	51
17	0	3	0	13	0	23	0	32	0	42	0	52	1	2	1	12	1	22	1	32	1	41	1	51
18	0	3	0	13	0	23	0	33	0	42	0	52	1	2	1	12	1	22	1	32	1	42	1	51
19	0	3	0	13	0	23	0	33	0	43	0	52	1	2	1	12	1	22	1	32	1	42	1	52
20	0	3	0	13	0	23	0	33	0	43	0	53	1	2	1	12	1	22	1	32	1	42	1	52
21	0	3	0	13	0	23	0	33	0	43	0	53	1	3	1	12	1	22	1	32	1	42	1	52
22	0	4	0	14	0	23	0	33	0	43	0	53	1	3	1	13	1	23	1	32	1	42	1	52
23	0	4	0	14	0	24	0	33	0	43	0	53	1	3	1	13	1	23	1	33	1	42	1	52
24	0	4	0	14	0	24	0	34	0	43	0	53	1	3	1	13	1	23	1	33	1	43	1	52
25	0	4	0	14	0	24	0	34	0	44	0	53	1	3	1	13	1	23	1	33	1	43	1	53
26	0	4	0	14	0	24	0	34	0	44	0	54	1	3	1	13	1	23	1	33	1	43	1	53
27	0	4	0	14	0	24	0	34	0	44	0	54	1	4	1	13	1	23	1	33	1	43	1	53
28	0	5	0	15	0	24	0	34	0	44	0	54	1	4	1	14	1	24	1	33	1	43	1	53
29	0	5	0	15	0	25	0	34	0	44	0	54	1	4	1	14	1	24	1	34	1	43	1	53
30	0	5	0	15	0	25	0	35	0	44	0	54	1	4	1	14	1	24	1	34	1	44	1	53
31	0	5	0	15	0	25	0	35	0	45	0	54	1	4	1	14	1	24	1	34	1	44	1	54
32	0	5	0	15	0	25	0	35	0	45	0	55	1	4	1	14	1	24	1	34	1	44	1	54
33	0	5	0	15	0	25	0	35	0	45	0	55	1	5	1	14	1	24	1	34	1	44	1	54
34	0	6	0	15	0	25	0	35	0	45	0	55	1	5	1	15	1	24	1	34	1	44	1	54
35	0	6	0	16	0	26	0	35	0	45	0	55	1	5	1	15	1	25	1	35	1	44	1	54
36	0	6	0	16	0	26	0	36	0	45	0	55	1	5	1	15	1	25	1	35	1	45	1	54
37	0	6	0	16	0	26	0	36	0	46	0	55	1	5	1	15	1	25	1	35	1	45	1	55
38	0	6	0	16	0	26	0	36	0	46	0	56	1	5	1	15	1	25	1	35	1	45	1	55
39	0	6	0	16	0	26	0	36	0	46	0	56	1	6	1	15	1	25	1	35	1	45	1	55
40	0	7	0	16	0	26	0	36	0	46	0	56	1	6	1	16	1	25	1	35	1	45	1	55
41	0	7	0	17	0	26	0	36	0	46	0	56	1	6	1	16	1	26	1	35	1	45	1	55
42	0	7	0	17	0	27	0	37	0	46	0	56	1	6	1	16	1	26	1	36	1	46	1	55
43	0	7	0	17	0	27	0	37	0	47	0	56	1	6	1	16	1	26	1	36	1	46	1	56
44	0	7	0	17	0	27	0	37	0	47	0	57	1	6	1	16	1	26	1	36	1	46	1	56
45	0	7	0	17	0	27	0	37	0	47	0	57	1	7	1	16	1	26	1	36	1	46	1	56
46	0	8	0	17	0	27	0	37	0	47	0	57	1	7	1	17	1	26	1	36	1	46	1	56
47	0	8	0	18	0	27	0	37	0	47	0	57	1	7	1	17	1	27	1	36	1	46	1	56
48	0	8	0	18	0	28	0	38	0	47	0	57	1	7	1	17	1	27	1	37	1	46	1	56
49	0	8	0	18	0	28	0	38	0	48	0	57	1	7	1	17	1	27	1	37	1	47	1	57
50	0	8	0	18	0	28	0	38	0	48	0	58	1	7	1	17	1	27	1	37	1	47	1	57
51	0	8	0	18	0	28	0	38	0	48	0	58	1	8	1	17	1	27	1	37	1	47	1	57
52	0	9	0	18	0	28	0	38	0	48	0	58	1	8	1	18	1	27	1	37	1	47	1	57
53	0	9	0	19	0	28	0	38	0	48	0	58	1	8	1	18	1	28	1	37	1	47	1	57
54	0	9	0	19	0	29	0	38	0	48	0	58	1	8	1	18	1	28	1	38	1	47	1	57
55	0	9	0	19	0	29	0	39	0	49	0	58	1	8	1	18	1	28	1	38	1	48	1	58
56	0	9	0	19	0	29	0	39	0	49	0	59	1	8	1	18	1	28	1	38	1	48	1	58
57	0	9	0	19	0	29	0	39	0	49	0	59	1	9	1	18	1	28	1	38	1	48	1	58
58	0	10	0	19	0	29	0	39	0	49	0	59	1	9	1	19	1	28	1	38	1	48	1	58
59	0	10	0	20	0	29	0	39	0	49	0	59	1	9	1	19	1	29	1	38	1	48	1	58

mean Solar	12 hr		13 hr		14 hr		15 hr		16 hr		17 hr		18 hr		19 hr		20 hr		21 hr		22 hr		23 hr	
min	m	s	m	s	m	s	m	s	m	s	m	s	m	s	m	s	m	s	m	s	m	s	m	s
0	1	58	2	8	2	18	2	28	2	38	2	48	2	57	3	7	3	17	3	27	3	37	3	47
1	1	58	2	8	2	18	2	28	2	38	2	48	2	58	3	7	3	17	3	27	3	37	3	47
2	1	59	2	9	2	18	2	28	2	38	2	48	2	58	3	8	3	18	3	27	3	37	3	47
3	1	59	2	9	2	19	2	28	2	38	2	48	2	58	3	8	3	18	3	28	3	37	3	47
4	1	59	2	9	2	19	2	29	2	38	2	48	2	58	3	8	3	18	3	28	3	38	3	47
5	1	59	2	9	2	19	2	29	2	39	2	48	2	58	3	8	3	18	3	28	3	38	3	48
6	1	59	2	9	2	19	2	29	2	39	2	49	2	58	3	8	3	18	3	28	3	38	3	48
7	1	59	2	9	2	19	2	29	2	39	2	49	2	59	3	8	3	18	3	28	3	38	3	48
8	2	0	2	9	2	19	2	29	2	39	2	49	2	59	3	9	3	18	3	28	3	38	3	48
9	2	0	2	10	2	20	2	29	2	39	2	49	2	59	3	9	3	19	3	29	3	38	3	48
10	2	0	2	10	2	20	2	30	2	39	2	49	2	59	3	9	3	19	3	29	3	39	3	48
11	2	0	2	10	2	20	2	30	2	40	2	49	2	59	3	9	3	19	3	29	3	39	3	49
12	2	0	2	10	2	20	2	30	2	40	2	50	2	59	3	9	3	19	3	29	3	39	3	49
13	2	0	2	10	2	20	2	30	2	40	2	50	3	0	3	9	3	19	3	29	3	39	3	49
14	2	1	2	10	2	20	2	30	2	40	2	50	3	0	3	10	3	19	3	29	3	39	3	49
15	2	1	2	11	2	21	2	30	2	40	2	50	3	0	3	10	3	20	3	29	3	39	3	49
16	2	1	2	11	2	21	2	31	2	40	2	50	3	0	3	10	3	20	3	30	3	40	3	49
17	2	1	2	11	2	21	2	31	2	41	2	50	3	0	3	10	3	20	3	30	3	40	3	50
18	2	1	2	11	2	21	2	31	2	41	2	51	3	0	3	10	3	20	3	30	3	40	3	50
19	2	1	2	11	2	21	2	31	2	41	2	51	3	1	3	10	3	20	3	30	3	40	3	50
20	2	2	2	11	2	21	2	31	2	41	2	51	3	1	3	11	3	20	3	30	3	40	3	50
21	2	2	2	12	2	21	2	31	2	41	2	51	3	1	3	11	3	21	3	30	3	40	3	50
22	2	2	2	12	2	22	2	32	2	41	2	51	3	1	3	11	3	21	3	31	3	41	3	50
23	2	2	2	12	2	22	2	32	2	42	2	51	3	1	3	11	3	21	3	31	3	41	3	51
24	2	2	2	12	2	22	2	32	2	42	2	52	3	1	3	11	3	21	3	31	3	41	3	51
25	2	2	2	12	2	22	2	32	2	42	2	52	3	2	3	11	3	21	3	31	3	41	3	51
26	2	3	2	12	2	22	2	32	2	42	2	52	3	2	3	12	3	21	3	31	3	41	3	51
27	2	3	2	13	2	22	2	32	2	42	2	52	3	2	3	12	3	22	3	31	3	41	3	51
28	2	3	2	13	2	23	2	32	2	42	2	52	3	2	3	12	3	22	3	32	3	41	3	51
29	2	3	2	13	2	23	2	33	2	43	2	52	3	2	3	12	3	22	3	32	3	42	3	52
30	2	3	2	13	2	23	2	33	2	43	2	53	3	2	3	12	3	22	3	32	3	42	3	52
31	2	3	2	13	2	23	2	33	2	43	2	53	3	3	3	12	3	22	3	32	3	42	3	52
32	2	4	2	13	2	23	2	33	2	43	2	53	3	3	3	13	3	22	3	32	3	42	3	52
33	2	4	2	14	2	23	2	33	2	43	2	53	3	3	3	13	3	23	3	32	3	42	3	52
34	2	4	2	14	2	24	2	33	2	43	2	53	3	3	3	13	3	23	3	33	3	42	3	52
35	2	4	2	14	2	24	2	34	2	44	2	53	3	3	3	13	3	23	3	33	3	43	3	52
36	2	4	2	14	2	24	2	34	2	44	2	54	3	3	3	13	3	23	3	33	3	43	3	53
37	2	4	2	14	2	24	2	34	2	44	2	54	3	4	3	13	3	23	3	33	3	43	3	53
38	2	5	2	14	2	24	2	34	2	44	2	54	3	4	3	14	3	23	3	33	3	43	3	53
39	2	5	2	15	2	24	2	34	2	44	2	54	3	4	3	14	3	24	3	33	3	43	3	53
40	2	5	2	15	2	25	2	34	2	44	2	54	3	4	3	14	3	24	3	34	3	43	3	53
41	2	5	2	15	2	25	2	35	2	44	2	54	3	4	3	14	3	24	3	34	3	44	3	53
42	2	5	2	15	2	25	2	35	2	45	2	55	3	4	3	14	3	24	3	34	3	44	3	54
43	2	5	2	15	2	25	2	35	2	45	2	55	3	5	3	14	3	24	3	34	3	44	3	54
44	2	6	2	15	2	25	2	35	2	45	2	55	3	5	3	15	3	24	3	34	3	44	3	54
45	2	6	2	16	2	25	2	35	2	45	2	55	3	5	3	15	3	25	3	34	3	44	3	54
46	2	6	2	16	2	26	2	35	2	45	2	55	3	5	3	15	3	25	3	35	3	44	3	54
47	2	6	2	16	2	26	2	36	2	45	2	55	3	5	3	15	3	25	3	35	3	45	3	54
48	2	6	2	16	2	26	2	36	2	46	2	55	3	5	3	15	3	25	3	35	3	45	3	55
49	2	6	2	16	2	26	2	36	2	46	2	56	3	6	3	15	3	25	3	35	3	45	3	55
50	2	7	2	16	2	26	2	36	2	46	2	56	3	6	3	16	3	25	3	35	3	45	3	55
51	2	7	2	17	2	26	2	36	2	46	2	56	3	6	3	16	3	26	3	35	3	45	3	55
52	2	7	2	17	2	27	2	36	2	46	2	56	3	6	3	16	3	26	3	36	3	45	3	55
53	2	7	2	17	2	27	2	37	2	46	2	56	3	6	3	16	3	26	3	36	3	46	3	55
54	2	7	2	17	2	27	2	37	2	47	2	56	3	6	3	16	3	26	3	36	3	46	3	56
55	2	7	2	17	2	27	2	37	2	47	2	57	3	7	3	16	3	26	3	36	3	46	3	56
56	2	8	2	17	2	27	2	37	2	47	2	57	3	7	3	17	3	26	3	36	3	46	3	56
57	2	8	2	18	2	27	2	37	2	47	2	57	3	7	3	17	3	27	3	36	3	46	3	56
58	2	8	2	18	2	28	2	37	2	47	2	57	3	7	3	17	3	27	3	37	3	46	3	56
59	2	8	2	18	2	28	2	38	2	47	2	57	3	7	3	17	3	27	3	37	3	47	3	56

APPENDIX L
LONGITUDE INTO TIME

Degrees

°	h m	°	h m	°	h m	°	h m
0	0 00	30	2 00	60	4 00	90	6 00
1	0 04	31	2 04	61	4 04	91	6 04
2	0 08	32	2 08	62	4 08	92	6 08
3	0 12	33	2 12	63	4 12	93	6 12
4	0 16	34	2 16	64	4 16	94	6 16
5	0 20	35	2 20	65	4 20	95	6 20
6	0 24	36	2 24	66	4 24	96	6 24
7	0 28	37	2 28	67	4 28	97	6 28
8	0 32	38	2 32	68	4 32	98	6 32
9	0 36	39	2 36	69	4 36	99	6 36
10	0 40	40	2 40	70	4 40	100	6 40
11	0 44	41	2 44	71	4 44	101	6 44
12	0 48	42	2 48	72	4 48	102	6 48
13	0 52	43	2 52	73	4 52	103	6 52
14	0 56	44	2 56	74	4 56	104	6 56
15	1 00	45	3 00	75	5 00	105	7 00
16	1 04	46	3 04	76	5 04	106	7 04
17	1 08	47	3 08	77	5 08	107	7 08
18	1 12	48	3 12	78	5 12	108	7 12
19	1 16	49	3 16	79	5 16	109	7 16
20	1 20	50	3 20	80	5 20	110	7 20
21	1 24	51	3 24	81	5 24	111	7 24
22	1 28	52	3 28	82	5 28	112	7 28
23	1 32	53	3 32	83	5 32	113	7 32
24	1 36	54	3 36	84	5 36	114	7 36
25	1 40	55	3 40	85	5 40	115	7 40
26	1 44	56	3 44	86	5 44	116	7 44
27	1 48	57	3 48	87	5 48	117	7 48
28	1 52	58	3 52	88	5 52	118	7 52
29	1 56	59	3 56	89	5 56	119	7 56

	Degrees						Minutes				
o	h	m	o	h	m	'	m	s	'	m	s
120	8	00	150	10	00	0	0	00	30	2	00
121	8	04	151	10	04	1	0	04	31	2	04
122	8	08	152	10	08	2	0	08	32	2	08
123	8	12	153	10	12	3	0	12	33	2	12
124	8	16	154	10	16	4	0	16	34	2	16
125	8	20	155	10	20	5	0	20	35	2	20
126	8	24	156	10	24	6	0	24	36	2	24
127	8	28	157	10	28	7	0	28	37	2	28
128	8	32	158	10	32	8	0	32	38	2	32
129	8	36	159	10	36	9	0	36	39	2	36
130	8	40	160	10	40	10	0	40	40	2	40
131	8	44	161	10	44	11	0	44	41	2	44
132	8	48	162	10	48	12	0	48	42	2	48
133	8	52	163	10	52	13	0	52	43	2	52
134	8	56	164	10	56	14	0	56	44	2	56
135	9	00	165	11	00	15	1	00	45	3	00
136	9	04	166	11	04	16	1	04	46	3	04
137	9	08	167	11	08	17	1	08	47	3	08
138	9	12	168	11	12	18	1	12	48	3	12
139	9	16	169	11	16	19	1	16	49	3	16
140	9	20	170	11	20	20	1	20	50	3	20
141	9	24	171	11	24	21	1	24	51	3	24
142	9	28	172	11	28	22	1	28	52	3	28
143	9	32	173	11	32	23	1	32	53	3	32
144	9	36	174	11	36	24	1	36	54	3	36
145	9	40	175	11	40	25	1	40	55	3	40
146	9	44	176	11	44	26	1	44	56	3	44
147	9	48	177	11	48	27	1	48	57	3	48
148	9	52	178	11	52	28	1	52	58	3	52
149	9	56	179	11	56	29	1	56	59	3	56

To use table: degrees of longitude are the left
row of each column; hours and minutes (labeled h
and m) adjoin them. In a similar fashion, minutes
of longitude are listed with minutes and seconds
of time (m and s) in the last two columns. Find
the time quantities for degrees and minutes (of
longitude) separately, then add to get the final
result of time.

Aries Libra	N S	Virgo Pisces	Aries Libra	N S	Virgo Pisces
0°00'	0 00	30°00'	6°00'	2 23	24°00'
10	0 04	50	10	2 27	50
20	0 08	40	20	2 31	40
30	0 12	30	30	2 35	30
40	0 15	20	40	2 39	20
50	0 19	10	50	2 43	10
1 00	0 23	29 00	7 00	2 47	23 00
10	0 27	50	10	2 51	50
20	0 31	40	20	2 55	40
30	0 35	30	30	2 59	30
40	0 39	20	40	3 03	20
50	0 43	10	50	3 07	10
2 00	0 47	28 00	8 00	3 11	22 00
10	0 51	50	10	3 15	50
20	0 55	40	20	3 19	40
30	1 00	30	30	3 23	30
40	1 04	20	40	3 27	20
50	1 08	10	50	3 31	10
3 00	1 12	27 00	9 00	3 34	21 00
10	1 16	50	10	3 38	50
20	1 20	40	20	3 42	40
30	1 24	30	30	3 46	30
40	1 28	20	40	3 50	20
50	1 32	10	50	3 54	10
4 00	1 36	26 00	10 00	3 58	20 00
10	1 39	50	10	4 02	50
20	1 44	40	20	4 06	40
30	1 48	30	30	4 10	30
40	1 51	20	40	4 14	20
50	1 55	10	50	4 18	10
5 00	1 59	25 00	11 00	4 22	19 00
10	2 03	50	10	4 26	50
20	2 07	40	20	4 29	40
30	2 11	30	30	4 33	30
40	2 15	20	40	4 37	20
50	2 19	10	50	4 41	10
6 00	2 23	24 00	12 00	4 45	18 00

Aries Libra	N S	Virgo Pisces	Aries Libra	N S	Virgo Pisces
12°00'	4 45	18°00'	18°00'	7 04	12°00'
10	4 49	50	10	7 08	50
20	4 53	40	20	7 12	40
30	4 57	30	30	7 15	30
40	5 01	20	40	7 19	20
50	5 04	10	50	7 23	10
13 00	5 08	17 00	19 00	7 27	11 00
10	5 12	50	10	7 31	50
20	5 16	40	20	7 34	40
30	5 20	30	30	7 38	30
40	5 24	20	40	7 41	20
50	5 28	10	50	7 45	10
14 00	5 32	16 00	20 00	7 49	10 00
10	5 36	50	10	7 53	50
20	5 40	40	20	7 56	40
30	5 43	30	30	8 00	30
40	5 47	20	40	8 03	20
50	5 51	10	50	8 07	10
15 00	5 55	15 00	21 00	8 11	9 00
10	5 59	50	10	8 15	50
20	6 03	40	20	8 19	40
30	6 06	30	30	8 22	30
40	6 10	20	40	8 26	20
50	6 14	10	50	8 30	10
16 00	6 18	14 00	22 00	8 34	8 00
10	6 22	50	10	8 38	50
20	6 26	40	20	8 42	40
30	6 29	30	30	8 45	30
40	6 33	20	40	8 49	20
50	6 37	10	50	8 53	10
17 00	6 41	13 00	23 00	8 56	7 00
10	6 45	50	10	9 00	50
20	6 49	40	20	9 04	40
30	6 52	30	30	9 08	30
40	6 56	20	40	9 12	20
50	7 00	10	50	9 16	10
18 00	7 04	12 00	24 00	9 19	6 00

Aries Libra	N S	Virgo Pisces	Taurus Scorp.	N S	Leo Aquar.
24°00'	9 19	6°00'	0°00'	11 28	30°00'
10	9 22	50	10	11 31	50
20	9 26	40	20	11 35	40
30	9 30	30	30	11 38	30
40	9 33	20	40	11 41	20
50	9 37	10	50	11 45	10
25 00	9 41	5 00	1 00	11 49	29 00
10	9 45	50	10	11 53	50
20	9 48	40	20	11 57	40
30	9 51	30	30	12 00	30
40	9 55	20	40	12 04	20
50	9 59	10	50	12 08	10
26 00	10 02	4 00	2 00	12 11	28 00
10	10 05	50	10	12 14	50
20	10 09	40	20	12 17	40
30	10 13	30	30	12 21	30
40	10 17	20	40	12 24	20
50	10 21	10	50	12 27	10
27 00	10 25	3 00	3 00	12 31	27 00
10	10 28	50	10	12 35	50
20	10 31	40	20	12 39	40
30	10 35	30	30	12 42	30
40	10 39	20	40	12 45	20
50	10 43	10	50	12 49	10
28 00	10 46	2 00	4 00	12 52	26 00
10	10 49	50	10	12 55	50
20	10 53	40	20	12 58	40
30	10 57	30	30	13 02	30
40	11 01	20	40	13 05	20
50	11 04	10	50	13 08	10
29 00	11 07	1 00	5 00	13 12	25 00
10	11 10	50	10	13 15	50
20	11 14	40	20	13 18	40
30	11 17	30	30	13 22	30
40	11 21	20	40	13 25	20
50	11 25	10	50	13 28	10
30 00	11 28	0 00	6 00	13 32	24 00

Taurus Scorp.	N S	Leo Aquar.	Taurus Scorp.	N S	Leo Aquar.
6°00'	13 32	24°00'	12°00'	15 26	18°00'
10	13 35	50	10	15 29	50
20	13 38	40	20	15 32	40
30	13 42	30	30	15 36	30
40	13 45	20	40	15 39	20
50	13 48	10	50	15 42	10
7 00	13 52	23 00	13 00	15 45	17 00
10	13 55	50	10	15 48	50
20	13 58	40	20	15 51	40
30	14 02	30	30	15 54	30
40	14 05	20	40	15 57	20
50	14 08	10	50	16 00	10
8 00	14 11	22 00	14 00	16 03	16 00
10	14 14	50	10	16 06	50
20	14 17	40	20	16 09	40
30	14 21	30	30	16 12	30
40	14 24	20	40	16 15	20
50	14 27	10	50	16 18	10
9 00	14 30	21 00	15 00	16 20	15 00
10	14 33	50	10	16 23	50
20	14 36	40	20	16 26	40
30	14 40	30	30	16 29	30
40	14 43	20	40	16 32	20
50	14 46	10	50	16 35	10
10 00	14 49	20 00	16 00	16 38	14 00
10	14 52	50	10	16 41	50
20	14 55	40	20	16 44	40
30	14 58	30	30	16 47	30
40	15 01	20	40	16 50	20
50	15 04	10	50	16 53	10
11 00	15 07	19 00	17 00	16 55	13 00
10	15 10	50	10	16 58	50
20	15 13	40	20	17 01	40
30	15 17	30	30	17 04	30
40	15 20	20	40	17 07	20
50	15 23	10	50	17 10	10
12 00	15 26	18 00	18 00	17 12	12 00

Taurus Scorp.	N S	Leo Aquar.	Taurus Scorp.	N S	Leo Aquar.
18°00'	17 12	12°00'	24°00'	18 47	6°00
10	17 15	50	10	18 49	50
20	17 18	40	20	18 51	40
30	17 21	30	30	18 54	30
40	17 24	20	40	18 56	20
50	17 27	10	50	18 59	10
19 00	17 29	11 00	25 00	19 01	5 00
10	17 32	50	10	19 03	50
20	17 35	40	20	19 06	40
30	17 37	30	30	19 08	30
40	17 39	20	40	19 10	20
50	17 42	10	50	19 13	10
20 00	17 45	10 00	26 00	19 16	4 00
10	17 47	50	10	19 18	50
20	17 51	40	20	19 21	40
30	17 53	30	30	19 23	30
40	17 55	20	40	19 25	20
50	17 58	10	50	19 28	10
21 00	18 01	9 00	27 00	19 30	3 00
10	18 03	50	10	19 32	50
20	18 05	40	20	19 35	40
30	18 08	30	30	19 37	30
40	18 11	20	40	19 39	20
50	18 13	10	50	19 42	10
22 00	18 16	8 00	28 00	19 44	2 00
10	18 19	50	10	19 46	50
20	18 22	40	20	19 48	40
30	18 24	30	30	19 51	30
40	18 26	20	40	19 53	20
50	18 29	10	50	19 55	10
23 00	18 32	7 00	29 00	19 57	1 00
10	18 35	50	10	19 59	50
20	18 38	40	20	20 01	40
30	18 40	30	30	20 03	30
40	18 42	20	40	20 05	20
50	18 45	10	50	20 07	10
24 00	18 47	6 00	30 00	20 09	0 00

Gemini Sagit.	N S		Cancer Capri.	Gemini Sagit.	N S		Cancer Capri.
0°00'	20	09	30°00'	6°00'	21	18	24°00'
10	20	11	50	10	21	20	50
20	20	13	40	20	21	22	40
30	20	15	30	30	21	24	30
40	20	17	20	40	21	26	20
50	20	19	10	50	21	27	10
1 00	20	22	29 00	7 00	21	29	23 00
10	20	24	50	10	21	31	50
20	20	26	40	20	21	33	40
30	20	28	30	30	21	34	30
40	20	30	20	40	21	35	20
50	20	32	10	50	21	37	10
2 00	20	34	28 00	8 00	21	39	22 00
10	20	36	50	10	21	41	50
20	20	38	40	20	21	43	40
30	20	40	30	30	21	44	30
40	20	42	20	40	21	45	20
50	20	44	10	50	21	47	10
3 00	20	46	27 00	9 00	21	48	21 00
10	20	48	50	10	21	50	50
20	20	50	40	20	21	52	40
30	20	52	30	30	21	53	30
40	20	54	20	40	21	54	20
50	20	55	10	50	21	56	10
4 00	20	57	26 00	10 00	21	57	20 00
10	20	59	50	10	21	59	50
20	21	01	40	20	22	00	40
30	21	03	30	30	22	02	30
40	21	05	20	40	22	03	20
50	21	07	10	50	22	05	10
5 00	21	08	25 00	11 00	22	06	19 00
10	21	10	50	10	22	08	50
20	21	11	40	20	22	09	40
30	21	13	30	30	22	10	30
40	21	15	20	40	22	11	20
50	21	16	10	50	22	13	10
6 00	21	18	24 00	12 00	22	14	18 00

Gemini Sagit.	N S	Cancer Capri.	Gemini Sagit.	N S	Cancer Capri.
12°00'	22 14	18°00'	19°00'	23 00	11°00'
20	22 17	40	30	23 02	30
40	22 20	20	20 00	23 04	10 00
13 00	22 22	17 00	30	23 06	30
20	22 25	40	21 00	23 08	9 00
40	22 28	20	30	23 10	30
14 00	22 30	16 00	22 00	23 12	8 00
20	22 32	40	30	23 14	30
40	22 34	20	23 00	23 16	7 00
15 00	22 36	15 00	30	23 18	30
20	22 38	40	24 00	23 19	6 00
40	22 40	20	30	23 21	30
16 00	22 42	14 00	25 00	23 22	5 00
20	22 44	40	26 00	23 23	4 00
40	22 47	20	27 00	23 24	3 00
17 00	22 49	13 00	28 00	23 25	2 00
30	22 52	30	29 00	23 26	1 00
18 00	22 54	12 00	30 00	23 27	0 00
30	22 57	30			

Examples of use of the table: (1) Find the declination of the Asc. which is at 15 Aries 20. Locate
the column headed Aries, find in that column 15°20'.
Opposite that figure, read 6 03; at the top of the
column, Aries is opposite N (for north), so the Asc.
declination will be 6N03. (Had it been for Libra
the declination would have been 6S03.) (2) Find the
declination of the M.C. at 2 Aquarius 25. Locate the
column headed Aquar.; find 2°20'. 25 is halfway
between 2°20' and 2°30', so the result will be the
figure between 19 39 and 19 37, or 19 38; Aquarius
is S (for south) so the M.C. declination is 19S38.

APPENDIX N

SYNOPSIS OF PLANETS CALCULATIONS

I. Start with *standard* time.
   (1) For any other, the extra hour (or hours) must be *subtracted*.
   (2) If L.M.T. is given (rare), convert birthplace longitude into time.
II. Determine equivalent Greenwich mean time—*E.G.M.T.*
   (1) To the time of birth add or subtract number of time zones (or the longitude equivalent) between the birthplace and Greenwich.
   (2) *Add* for *west* longitude; *subtract* for *east.*
   (3) Draw time diagram if need be.
III. Work with noon of date of E.G.M.T., and determine E.G.M.T. *Interval.*
   (1) If E.G.M.T. is *P.M.,* interval will be a *plus* (forward from noon) interval.
   (2) If E.G.M.T. is *A.M.,* interval will be a *minus* interval (back from noon).
   (3) For midnight ephemerides work with nearer midnight, and reverse (1) and (2).
IV. Find E.G.M.T. position of planets and declinations.
   (1) Find *proportional motion,* and add or subtract from given noon or midnight position.
   (2) Add or subtract according to whether the interval is plus or minus to or from the listed noon (or midnight) position.

SYNOPSIS OF HOUSE CUSP CALCULATIONS

I. Determine local sidereal time (L.S.T.).
   (1) Use same noon (or midnight) as for planets, and find listed sidereal time in ephemeris.
   (2) Add or subtract (according to plus or minus) E.G.M.T. Int.
   (3) Likewise add or subtract correction factor (for changing solar mean into sidereal time) for interval.
   (4) Determine longitude of birthplace and change into time; add or subtract;
     (a) Add for east; subtract for west.

II. Locate L.S.T. at birthplace latitude in a table of houses, and find cusp positions.

    (1) For southern latitudes: add 12 hours to the L.S.T., use cusp positions for that time, but use opposite zodiacal signs.

III. Compute Part of Fortune.

    (1) Part of Fortune is same relative position to the Asc. as the Moon is to the Sun.

IV. The steps in double interpolation of house cusp positions are as follows:

    (1) The birthplace latitude is the *given latitude;* listed on either side of it, in the table of houses, is a *lesser latitude* and a *greater latitude.* Likewise, the L.S.T. is the *given time;* listed in the tables is a *lesser time* and a *greater time.*

    (2) Locate in the tables the page for the lesser latitude and underline the lesser time. Also underline the lesser time in the table for the greater latitude.

    (3) On the work sheet, construct a new table for the given latitude at each of the two listed times. Each table will show the following:

THE LESSER TIME

    diff. (d): the difference of each cusp position of the six houses between its position at the lesser latitude and its position at the greater latitude. The difference may be plus or minus according to whether the position of the particular cusp moved forward or backward in the zodiac.

    lat. pos.: the cusp positions at the lesser latitude.

    prop. (c): is the proportion of the differences above, and is added or subtracted as the difference is plus or minus to or from the lesser latitude positions, to give the positions at the given latitude.

THE GREATER TIME

    same

    (4) *c* is solved with the usual proportion, where:

        a is the difference between the lesser latitude and the given latitude (the partial difference).

        b is the difference between the lesser latitude and the greater latitude (the whole difference).

        c is the unknown.

        d is the difference as described above.

(5) A third table is set up to show the positions at the given time:

THE GIVEN TIME

diff. (d) is the difference of each cusp position between its position at the lesser time and its position at the greater time (at the given latitude as computed in the two previous tables).

lat. pos.: the cusp positions at the lesser time (at the given latitude).

prop. (c): is the proportion of the difference above. Since the difference is always plus, the proportion is always added to the position at the lesser time to give the cusp positions at the given time at the given latitude.

(6) The proportion is solved where:

a is the difference between the lesser time and the given time (the partial difference).

b is the difference between the lesser time and the greater time (the whole difference).

c is the unknown.

d is the difference above.

(7) For the other six houses not in the tables, use the same positions as computed for the first six, but for each opposing house use the opposite zodiacal sign.

SYNOPSIS OF PROGRESSIONS CALCULATIONS

I. Progressions are reckoned at the rate of a day for a year.

(1) A day in the ephemeris is equal to a year in the native's life.

II. Determine the Zero P.E.D.

(1) The P.E.D. (Progression Ephemeris Date) is the date during the year that coincides with Noon or Midnight; it is used to avoid calculating planet positions.

(2) Start with the E.G.M.T. Convert the E.G.M.T. Interval to months and days.

(a) Divide the Interval by 2: equals months. Convert the remainder to minutes and divide by 4: equals additional days.

Or

(b) Use proportion, where b = 24, d = 365

(3) If E.G.M.T. Interval is *minus*, ADD the results of (2) to the E.G.M.T. date of birth to get P.E.D. If Interval is *plus*, SUBTRACT.

(4) Draw a time diagram to avoid confusion.

III. Progress to the desired year.

  (1) Subtract year of Zero P.E.D. from desired year.

    (a) Year of Zero P.E.D. may differ from year of birth.

  (2) Convert the results of (1) into days, and count ahead in the ephemeris that many days.

  (3) Use the planet positions directly as shown in the ephemeris and enter them in the outer wheel of the chart.

    (a) Use red for all progressed data.

  (4) Use the declinations also as given in the ephemeris

  (5) Note on the chart the year of the progression and the equivalent date.

  (6) To find the progressed positions and declinations of the M.C. and Asc.:

    (a) Determine the M.C.C. (Constant) by finding in the natal chart how far ahead or behind the Sun the M.C. is.

    (b) Take the progressed Sun position and use the M.C.C. to find the position of the progressed M.C.

    (c) Find the progressed M.C. position in a table of houses for the birth latitude (under 10th house). Opposite this find the progressed Asc. Interpolate if necessary.

    (d) Use Appendix M to find the declinations of the progressed M.C. and Asc.

IV. List Rates of Motion of progressed positions and declinations.

  (1) Progressed date for two successive years is needed.

  (2) Subtract planet position of earlier date from that of later to get progressed motion for one year (or one day in ephemeris).

  (3) Do same with declinations.

  (4) The position or declination for any date between the two P.E.D.s may now be found by simple proportion.

    (a) It is usually sufficient to calculate mentally to the nearest month.

APPENDIX O
THE ASPECTS

ASPECT	KEYWORD	SYMBOL	DEGREES APART
Conjunction	Prominence	☌	0
Semi-sextile	Growth	⌄	30
Semi-square	Friction	∠	45
Sextile	Opportunity	✳	60
Square	Obstacle	□	90
Trine	Luck	△	120
Sesquiquadrate	Agitation	⚎	135
Quincunx (or Inconjunct)	Expansion	⚻	150
Opposition	Conflict	☍	180
Parallel	Intensity	‖	-

DEGREES OF ORB

ASPECTS	PLANETS	PLANETS LUMIN.	TYPE OF HOUSE ANGLE	SUC.	CAD.
☌ ☍	10	+ 3	+ 2	-	- 2
□ △	8	+ 2	+ 2	-	- 2
✳	6	+ 1	+ 1	-	- 1
∠ ⚎	4	+ 1	+ 1	-	- 1
⌄ ⚻	2	+ 1	+ 1	-	- 1

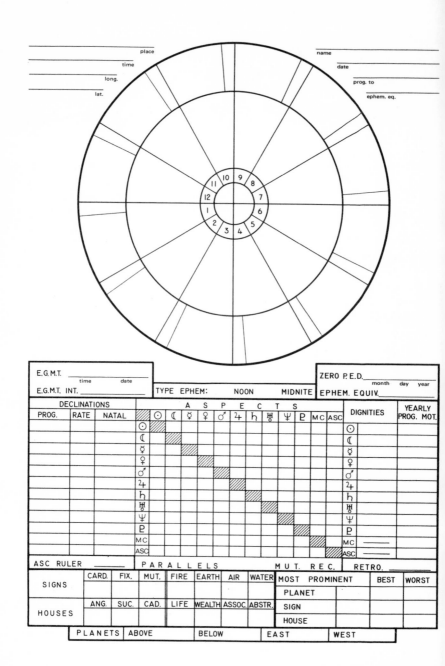

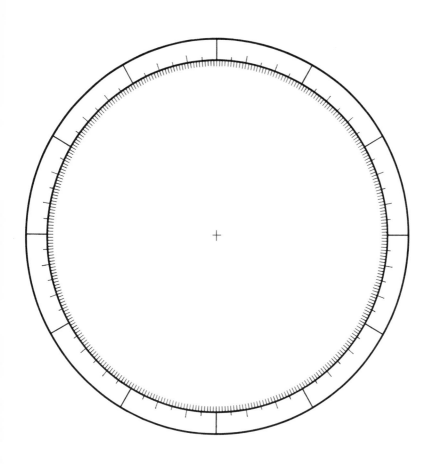

THE 360° CHART

APPENDIX R
DAYS OF THE YEAR NUMBERED

Day	Jan	Feb	Mar	Apr	May	Jun	Jul	Aug	Sep	Oct	Nov	Dec
1	1	32	60	91	121	152	182	213	244	274	305	335
2	2	33	61	92	122	153	183	214	245	275	306	336
3	3	34	62	93	123	154	184	215	246	276	307	337
4	4	35	63	94	124	155	185	216	247	277	308	338
5	5	36	64	95	125	156	186	217	248	278	309	339
6	6	37	65	96	126	157	187	218	249	279	310	340
7	7	38	66	97	127	158	188	219	250	280	311	341
8	8	39	67	98	128	159	189	220	251	281	312	342
9	9	40	68	99	129	160	190	221	252	282	313	343
10	10	41	69	100	130	161	191	222	253	283	314	344
11	11	42	70	101	131	162	192	223	254	284	315	345
12	12	43	71	102	132	163	193	224	255	285	316	346
13	13	44	72	103	133	164	194	225	256	286	317	347
14	14	45	73	104	134	165	195	226	257	287	318	348
15	15	46	74	105	135	166	196	227	258	288	319	349
16	16	47	75	106	136	167	197	228	259	289	320	350
17	17	48	76	107	137	168	198	229	260	290	321	351
18	18	49	77	108	138	169	199	230	261	291	322	352
19	19	50	78	109	139	170	200	231	262	292	323	353
20	20	51	79	110	140	171	201	232	263	293	324	354
21	21	52	80	111	141	172	202	233	264	294	325	355
22	22	53	81	112	142	173	203	234	265	295	326	356
23	23	54	82	113	143	174	204	235	266	296	327	357
24	24	55	83	114	144	175	205	236	267	297	328	358
25	25	56	84	115	145	176	206	237	268	298	329	359
26	26	57	85	116	146	177	207	238	269	299	330	360
27	27	58	86	117	147	178	208	239	270	300	331	361
28	28	59	87	118	148	179	209	240	271	301	332	362
29	29		88	119	149	180	210	241	272	302	333	363
30	30		89	120	150	181	211	242	273	303	334	364
31	31		90		151		212	243		304		365

SECOND YEAR

Day	Jan	Feb	Mar	Apr	May	Jun	Jul	Aug	Sep	Oct	Nov	Dec
1	366	397	425	456	486	517	547	578	609	639	670	700
2	367	398	426	457	487	518	548	579	610	640	671	701
3	368	399	427	458	488	519	549	580	611	641	672	702
4	369	400	428	459	489	520	550	581	612	642	673	703
5	370	401	429	460	490	521	551	582	613	643	674	704
6	371	402	430	461	491	522	552	583	614	644	675	705
7	372	403	431	462	492	523	553	584	615	645	676	706
8	373	404	432	463	493	524	554	585	616	646	677	707
9	374	405	433	464	494	525	555	586	617	647	678	708
10	375	406	434	465	495	526	556	587	618	648	679	709
11	376	407	435	466	496	527	557	588	619	649	680	710
12	377	408	436	467	497	528	558	589	620	650	681	711
13	378	409	437	468	498	529	559	590	621	651	682	712
14	379	410	438	469	499	530	560	591	622	652	683	713
15	380	411	439	470	500	531	561	592	623	653	684	714
16	381	412	440	471	501	532	562	593	624	654	685	715
17	382	413	441	472	502	533	563	594	625	655	686	716
18	383	414	442	473	503	534	564	595	626	656	687	717
19	384	415	443	474	504	535	565	596	627	657	688	718
20	385	416	444	475	505	536	566	597	628	658	689	719
21	386	417	445	476	506	537	567	598	629	659	690	720
22	387	418	446	477	507	538	568	599	630	660	691	721
23	388	419	447	478	508	539	569	600	631	661	692	722
24	389	420	448	479	509	540	570	601	632	662	693	723
25	390	421	449	480	510	541	571	602	633	663	694	724
26	391	422	450	481	511	542	572	603	634	664	695	725
27	392	423	451	482	512	543	573	604	635	665	696	726
28	393	424	452	483	513	544	574	605	636	666	697	727
29	394		453	484	514	545	575	606	637	667	698	728
30	395		454	485	515	546	576	607	638	668	699	729
31	396		455		516		577	608		669		730

482

APPENDIX S
LIST OF PLANET DIGNITIES

	Home	Detriment
SUN	Leo	Aquarius
MOON	Cancer	Capricorn
MERCURY	Gemini	Sagittarius
	Virgo	Pisces
VENUS	Taurus	Scorpio
	Libra	Aries
MARS	Aries	Libra
	Scorpio	Taurus
JUPITER	Sagittarius	Gemini
	Pisces	Virgo
SATURN	Capricorn	Cancer
	Aquarius	Leo
URANUS	Aquarius	Leo
NEPTUNE	Pisces	Virgo
PLUTO	Scorpio	Taurus

	Exaltation	Fall
SUN	Aries	Libra
MOON	Taurus	Scorpio
MERCURY	Aquarius	Leo
VENUS	Pisces	Virgo
MARS	Capricorn	Cancer
JUPITER	Cancer	Capricorn
SATURN	Libra	Aries
URANUS	Gemini	Sagittarius
NEPTUNE	Sagittarius	Gemini
PLUTO	Leo	Aquarius

APPENDIX T
THE DECANATES AND THEIR RULERS

ARIES (MARS)
  First decanate $(0^o - 9^o)$ Mars
  Second decanate $(10^o - 19^o)$ Sun
  Third decanate $(20^o - 29^o)$ Jupiter

TAURUS (VENUS)
  First decanate $(0^o - 9^o)$ Venus
  Second decanate $(10^o - 19^o)$ Mercury
  Third decanate $(20^o - 29^o)$ Saturn

GEMINI (MERCURY)
  First decanate $(0^o - 9^o)$ Mercury
  Second decanate $(10^o - 19^o)$ Venus
  Third decanate $(20^o - 29^o)$ Saturn, Uranus

CANCER (MOON)
  First decanate $(0^o - 9^o)$ Moon
  Second decanate $(10^o - 19^o)$ Mars, Pluto
  Third decanate $(20^o - 29^o)$ Jupiter, Neptune

LEO (SUN)
  First decanate $(0^o - 9^o)$ Sun
  Second decanate $(10^o - 19^o)$ Jupiter
  Third decanate $(20^o - 29^o)$ Mars

VIRGO (MERCURY)
  First decanate $(0^o - 9^o)$ Mercury
  Second decanate $(10^o - 19^o)$ Saturn
  Third decanate $(20^o - 29^o)$ Venus

LIBRA (VENUS)
    First decanate (0° - 9°)   Venus
    Second decanate (10° - 19°)   Saturn, Uranus
    Third decanate (20° - 29°)   Mercury

SCORPIO (MARS, PLUTO)
    First decanate (0° - 9°)   Mars, Pluto
    Second decanate (10° - 19°)   Jupiter, Neptune
    Third decanate (20° - 29°)   Moon

SAGITTARIUS (JUPITER)
    First decanate (0° - 9°)   Jupiter
    Second decanate (10° - 19°)   Mars
    Third decanate (20° - 29°)   Sun

CAPRICORN (SATURN)
    First decanate (0° - 9°)   Saturn
    Second decanate (10° - 19°)   Venus
    Third decanate (20° - 29°)   Mercury

AQUARIUS (SATURN, URANUS)
    First decanate (0° - 9°)   Saturn, Uranus
    Second decanate (10° - 19°)   Mercury
    Third decanate (20° - 29°)   Venus

PISCES (JUPITER, NEPTUNE)
    First decanate (0° - 9°)   Jupiter, Neptune
    Second decanate (10° - 19°)   Moon
    Third decanate (20° - 29°)   Mars, Pluto

APPENDIX U
TABLE OF MUTUAL RECEPTIONS

SUN IN:	IN LEO OR ARIES*
Aries	Mars
Taurus	Venus or Moon*
Gemini	Mercury or Uranus*
Cancer	Moon or Jupiter*
Leo	Pluto*
Virgo	Mercury
Libra	Venus or Saturn*
Scorpio	Mars or Pluto
Sagittarius	Jupiter or Neptune*
Capricorn	Saturn or Mars*
Aquarius	Saturn or Uranus or Mercury*
Pisces	Jupiter or Neptune or Venus*

MOON IN:	IN CANCER OR TAURUS*
Aries	Mars
Taurus	Venus
Gemini	Mercury or Uranus*
Cancer	Jupiter*
Leo	Pluto*
Virgo	Mercury
Libra	Venus or Saturn*
Scorpio	Mars or Pluto
Sagittarius	Jupiter or Neptune*
Capricorn	Saturn or Mars*
Aquarius	Saturn or Uranus or Mercury*
Pisces	Jupiter or Neptune or Venus*

MERCURY IN: IN GEMINI OR VIRGO OR
                           AQUARIUS*

    Aries   Mars
    Taurus   Venus
    Gemini   Uranus*
    Cancer   Jupiter*
    Leo   Pluto*
    Libra   Venus or Saturn*
    Scorpio   Mars or Pluto
    Sagittarius   Jupiter or Neptune*
    Capricorn   Saturn or Mars*
    Aquarius   Saturn or Uranus
    Pisces   Jupiter or Neptune or Venus*

VENUS IN: IN TAURUS OR LIBRA OR
                           PISCES*

    Aries   Mars
    Gemini   Uranus*
    Cancer   Jupiter*
    Leo   Pluto*
    Libra   Saturn*
    Scorpio   Mars or Pluto
    Sagittarius   Jupiter or Neptune*
    Capricorn   Saturn or Mars*
    Aquarius   Saturn or Uranus
    Pisces   Jupiter or Neptune

MARS IN: IN ARIES OR SCORPIO OR
                           CAPRICORN*

    Gemini   Uranus*
    Cancer   Jupiter*
    Leo   Pluto*
    Libra   Saturn*
    Scorpio   Pluto
    Sagittarius   Jupiter or Neptune*
    Capricorn   Saturn or Mars*
    Aquarius   Saturn or Uranus
    Pisces   Jupiter or Neptune

```
JUPITER IN:              IN SAGITTARIUS OR PISCES
                         OR CANCER*

    Gemini               Uranus*
    Leo                  Pluto*
    Libra                Saturn*
    Scorpio              Pluto
    Sagittarius          Neptune*
    Capricorn            Saturn
    Aquarius             Saturn or Uranus
    Pisces               Neptune

  SATURN IN:             IN CAPRICORN OR LIBRA OR
                         AQUARIUS*

    Gemini               Uranus*
    Leo                  Pluto*
    Scorpio              Pluto
    Sagittarius          Neptune*
    Aquarius             Uranus
    Pisces               Neptune

  URANUS IN:             IN AQUARIUS OR GEMINI

    Leo                  Pluto*
    Scorpio              Pluto
    Sagittarius          Neptune*
    Pisces               Neptune

  NEPTUNE IN:            IN PISCES OR SAGITTARIUS

    Leo                  Pluto*
    Scorpio              Pluto
```

Mutual reception is when two planets are in each other's home and/or exalted positions. In this table, to differentiate, any mutual reception as the result of an exalted position is starred. For example: if the Sun is in Taurus (the Moon's exalted position), and the Moon in Leo (the Sun's home position), the Moon is starred to indicate the exaltation.

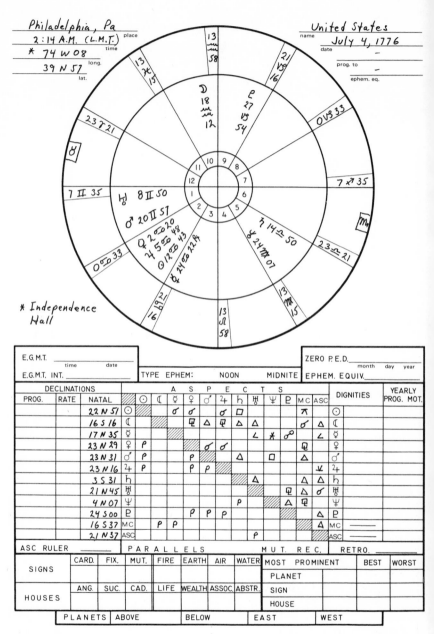

From *Astrology: 30 Years Research* by Doris Chase Doane—with her kind permission.

Stockholm, Sweden
1:20 A.M. _time_
18° 3' E _long._
59° 20 N _lat._

"INGRID" _name_
Sept. 5, 1931 _date_
Aug 31, 1972 _prog. to_
Oct 16, 1931 _ephem. eq._

Grand Square

E.G.M.T.	0:20 A.M	9-5-31				ZERO P.E.D.	Aug 31 1931		
	time	_date_					_month_ _day_ _year_		
E.G.M.T. INT.	20 min.	TYPE EPHEM:	NOON	(MIDNITE)	EPHEM. EQUIV.	9-5-31			

DECLINATIONS			A	S	P	E	C	T	S					DIGNITIES		YEARLY PROG. MOT.
PROG.	RATE	NATAL	☉	☽	☿	♀	♂	♃	♄	♅	♆	♇	MC	ASC		
8 S 27	22'	7 N 16	☉	□	☌	☌	∠	⚼	△		☌					☉		60'
28 S 22	13	26 N 16	☽		□	□	⊒	✳		∠	□	∠		✳	✳	☽		13° 31'
6 S 42	44	3 N 45	☿			☌	∠	⚼	△		☌			⚼		☿	Home	1° 42
11 S 22	27	8 N 53	♀				∠	⚼								♀	Fall	1° 15
18 S 2	12	8 S 27	♂			‖		□	☍	∠	□					♂	Detr.	42'
15 N 56	-2	17 N 59	♃					△			△	☌		△		♃		9'
22 S 21	0	22 S 19	♄				MR			□	⚒	☍				♄	Home	2'
6 N 8	-1	6 N 43	♅	‖						□	□	☌		♅		♅		-2'
9 N 34	0	10 N 4	♆								∠	⚻	⚼	♆	Detr.		2
22 N 3	0	22 N 6	♇				MR	‖							♇		0
16 N 54	17	2 S 41	MC											△	MC	———		60'
10 N 57	-13	18 N 20	ASC					‖							ASC	———		37

ASC RULER	☉	PARALLELS			MUT. REC.		RETRO.	☿ ♄ ♅

SIGNS	CARD.	FIX.	MUT.	FIRE	EARTH	AIR	WATER	MOST PROMINENT		BEST	WORST
	4 MC.	1 Asc.	5	2 M.C. Asc	5	2	1	PLANET	☽	♃	♂
HOUSES	ANG.	SUC.	CAD.	LIFE	WEALTH	ASSOC.	ABSTR.	SIGN	♍	♌	♎
	3	2	5	1	3	4	2	HOUSE	3	1	4

PLANETS	ABOVE	3	BELOW	7	EAST	8	WEST	2

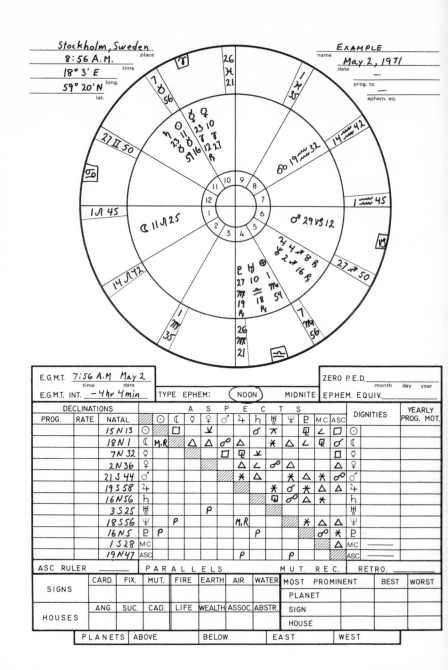

ENCYCLOPEDIA OF PLANETS, SIGNS, AND HOUSES

SUN ☉
864,000 miles in diameter
96.6 million miles from the earth
28 days in each sign
Rules LEO

Principal keywords:
  (Positive)   (Negative)
THE BASIC PERSON (THE   ARROGANCE
INDIVIDUALITY)   CONCEIT
VITALITY   EGOTISM
POWER
DIGNITY
CONFIDENCE

Other rulerships:
     achievement, desire for
     advancement
     ambition
     authority
     bosses
     bragging
     brokers
     celebrities
     children (in general)
     creativity, ability to create
     entertainment
     fame, famous people
     father
     gambling: places, equipment, persons

```
gold
honor
husband
influence
leaders
life, principle of life
lions
male sex in general
omnipotence
oxygen
pleasures, things of pleasure
politics, politicians
pride
speculation
stage, the
status
Sunday
```

MOON ☾
2,160 miles in diameter
237,000 miles mean distance from earth
Time in orbit 29½ days
2½ days in each sign
Rules CANCER

Principal keywords:
  (Positive)   (Negative)
THE SUBCONSCIOUS   MOODS
REACTION   INCONSISTENCY
RESPONSE   OVERSENSITIVITY
DOMESTIC MATTERS   INTROVERSION
EMOTIONS

Other rulerships:
    adaptability
    allergies
    baptism
    baths

```
beaches
beverages
boats, boating
breasts
childhood, childhood environment
cleaning
collections, collecting
common people
crowds
cycles
emotional persons
emotions
environment
evening
females in general
fish, fishing, markets, equipment
fluctuation
fluids
gestation
glass, glassware, glass factories
insomnia
instincts
laundry, laundries, laundry machines
liquids
lunacy
masses, the
mother
navigation, navigators
poultry
public: dealings, commodities, opinion
sea, seamen
sensitivity
silver
sleep
stomach
water, watery places, occupations etc.
wife
women
```

MERCURY   ☿
3,000 miles in diameter
36.2 million miles mean distance from the sun
Time of orbit 88 days
7 days in each sign
Rules GEMINI and VIRGO

Principal keywords:
  (Positive)   (Negative)
THE CONSCIOUS MIND   CRITICISM
COMMUNICATION   RESTLESSNESS
INTELLECTUAL AND   INDECISIVNESS
EDUCATIONAL MATTERS   NERVOUSNESS
EXPRESSION   TENSION

Other rulerships:
      accounts, accounting
      accuracy
      adaptability
      advertising
      advice
      agencies, agents
      agreements (written)
      air, air travel
      amnesia
      animals (of all kinds)
      announcers
      apprentices, apprenticeship
      architects
      asthma
      auditors
      authors
      books: stores, binderies
      bookkeepers
      breath
      brothers and sisters
      cabs
      catalogues
      charts
      clerks

computers, computer operators
concentration
conferences
conversation
cousins
craftsmen
critics
dictionaries
diet
doctors, doctoring
employees
hearing
hygiene
ideas
information
insomnia
intellectuals
journalists, journalism
languages
letters, letter writing
libraries
magazines
mentors
names
neighbors, the neighborhood
nerves, the nervous system
news
pencils, pens
pneumonia
post offices
printers, printing
publishers, publishing
reading
schools
speech, speaking
telephones
textbooks
travel (local or short range)
writers, writing

VENUS   ♀
7,600 miles in diameter
67.2 million miles mean distance from the sun
Time of orbit 224.7 days
19 days in each sign
Rules TAURUS and LIBRA

Principal keywords:
  (Positive)   (Negative)
LOVE   INDOLENCE
HARMONY   LAZINESS
ARTISTIC PURSUITS   WEAKNESS
BEAUTY
GENTLENESS

Other rulerships:
      actors, actresses, acting
      adolescence
      affection
      alimony
      architecture
      armistices
      art: objects, dealers, museums
      artists
      attraction
      ballet
      beauty
      bedrooms
      blood (venous)
      botany
      brides, bridegrooms
      candy
      clubs, social
      complexion
      dance, dancing
      desires
      drama
      earnings
      engagement (for marriage)
      entertainment

eroticism
esthetics
etiquette
fashion
feminism
flowers
furniture, furnishings
gems
genitals (internal)
gentleness
guests
harmony
hobbies
holidays
immodesty
indulgence
innocence
interior decorators
leisure
love affairs, lovers
marriage: the mate
money, money matters
music: halls, instruments, ability
ornaments
ovaries
paint, painting
pleasures, things of pleasure
protocol
recreation
sculpture
skin
social functions
society
treasurers, treasuries
valets
vanity
veins
venereal diseases
women

MARS   ♂
4,200 miles in diameter
141.6 million miles mean distance from the sun
Time of orbit 687 days
60 days in each sign
Rules ARIES; co-ruler of SCORPIO (with Pluto)

Principal keywords:
  (Positive)   (Negative)
ENERGY   AGGRESSIVENESS
HEAT   RECKLESSNESS
MECHANICAL ABILITY   ACCIDENTS
ACTIVITY   IRRITABILITY

Other rulerships:
     accidents
     activity
     adrenalin
     adventures
     antagonism
     arguments
     armed forces (Army, Navy)
     assault
     assertiveness
     athletes
     battles
     belligerence
     bladder
     blemishes (skin)
     boisterousness
     boxers, boxing
     bravery
     brutality
     burglars, burglary
     burns
     carpenters
     challenge
     chemistry
     confidence (self)
     cooks, cooking

courage
crime, criminals
cruelty
cuts
dentists
druggists, drugstores
emergencies
engineers, engineering (in general)
enthusiasm
excitement
exercise
exertion
explosives, explosions
fire, firemen
force
foundries
friction
garnets
genitals (external)
guns, gunmen
head, headaches
heroes
impatience
incisions
inflammation
injuries
instruments, sharp for cutting; knives
iron, steel
lust
machinery, machines, machinists
males
military, military men
munitions
murder
muscles, muscle system
operations (surgical)
passion
patriotism
pornography
procreative act

rage
red
scalds
sports
temper (loss of)
theft, thieves
tobacco
torture
Tuesday
violence
wars, warfare, warriers
weapons
wrecks

JUPITER   ♃
89,000 miles in diameter
483 million miles mean distance from the sun
Time of orbit 11.86 years
12 months in each sign
Rules SAGITTARIUS; co-ruler of PISCES (with Neptune)

Principal keywords:
  (Positive)   (Negative)
ABUNDANCE   EXCESS
BENEVOLENCE   EXTRAVAGANCE
OPTIMISM   EXTREMISM
HAPPINESS
DEVELOPMENT

Other rulerships:
     abscesses
     accumulation
     acquisition
     adrenal glands
     advantages
     affluence
     altars

applause
attorneys
auditors, auditing
awards
banks, bankers, banking
benefactors
Bible
blessings
blood (in general)
brokers
capitalism, capitalists
carelessness
censors
ceremonies
cheer, cheerful
chivalry
church, church affairs, churchmen
civilians
clergymen
colleges and universities, students
commerce
courts (of law)
customers
customs (mores)
customs (imports)
dignity
doctors, doctoring
earnings (wages)
education (higher)
embezzlement, embezzlers
encyclopedias
enlargement
ethics
etiquette
exaggeration
excellence
expansion
expensive
extravagance
fat

fines
foreign countries
fortune (good)
gain
generosity
gluttony
gratitude
hospitality
idealists
inheritances
integrity
judges, judicial system
juries
law, lawyers
passports
peace
philosophy, philosophers
physicians
pride
professional people of all kinds
prosperity
publishers, publishing
races (horse)
religion
teachers (college)
textbooks
theologians
Thursday
tin
travel (foreign)
trust
truth
voyages (long)
wealth, wealthy persons
writings that are published

SATURN   ♄
75,000 miles in diameter
886 million miles mean distance from the sun
Time of orbit 29.5 years
2½ years in each sign
Rules CAPRICORN; co-ruler of AQUARIUS (with
Uranus)

Principal keywords:
(Positive)   (Negative)
PATIENCE   LIMITATION
COOLNESS   COLD
CAUTION   PESSIMISM
ORGANIZATION   LOSS
ASPIRATION   DEPRESSION

Other rulerships:
     aches (dull)
     adhesives
     agriculture
     animosity
     anxieties
     apprehension
     avarice
     bankruptcy
     bereavement
     bones (the skeleton as a whole)
     boredom
     burdens
     celibacy
     chiropractors, chiropractic
     concrete
     conservatives, conservation
     constipation
     covetousness
     crystals, crystallization
     darkness
     debts, debtors
     deceit, deception
     dryness

earth, products of the earth
elderly persons, elders
encumbrances
endurance
envy
failures
farms, farmers, farming
fatigue
fear
feces
forts, fortification
foundations
frigidity
frost
funerals
gloom
grain, granaries
grief
grudges
handicaps
horror
ice
integrety
invalids
isolation
knees
labor, the laboring class, hard labor,
  place of labor
lack
lead (metal)
leather goods; workers
martyrs, martyrdom
masonry
mines, mining
misers
misery
mountains, mountainous places
night workers
obedience
old, old age, elderly people

orderliness
organization, organizers, ability to
   organize
permanance
perseverance
politics, politicians
real estate, realty-agents
relics
resistance
Satan
Saturday
secrets, secret feelings, secret matters
selfishness
senility
seriousness
underground
unhappiness
unluckiness
work of all kinds, workers

URANUS ♅
29,300 miles in diameter
1,783 million miles mean distance from the sun
Time of orbit 84.02 years
7 years in each sign
Co-ruler of AQUARIUS (with Saturn)

Principal keywords:
 (Positive)   (Negative)
CHANGE   ECCENTRICITY
ORIGINALITY   REBELLION
INDIVIDUALITY   DISRUPTION
INVENTIVENESS   WILFULNESS

Other rulerships:
     abnormalities (general and physical)
     abruptness
     accidents

agitation, agitators
air
airplanes, airports
anarchy
animation
astrology, astrologers
automation
automobiles
bastards
bicycles, bicycling
bombers, bombs
broadcasting
catastrophes
cinema
cranks (people)
crises
curiosity
deviation
different, that which is
discovery, discovering
disorganization, disorder
earthquakes
electricity, electricians
electric products
electronics
emancipation
emphysema
eviction
expeditions
experiments
exploration
explosives
fanatics
freaks
freelancing
fugitives
healing (by faith or unorthodox methods)
hippies
homosexuals
iconoclasts

idiosyncrasies
inventions, inventors
machinery
magnetism, magnets
miracles
miscarriages
panic
paradoxes
psychiatrists, psychologists
radio: technicians, operators, broadcasting
revolution
socialism (political)
suicides
television
tornadoes
unusual
wires (electric or telephone)
X-ray: technicians, machines

NEPTUNE   ♆
27,700 miles in diameter
2,793 million miles mean distance from the sun
Time of orbit 164.8 years
14½ years in each sign
Co-ruler of PISCES (with Jupiter)

Principal keywords:
 (Positive)   (Negative)
IDEALISM   VAGUENESS
INTUITION   IMPRACTICALITY
IMAGINATION   DECEPTION
CREATIVITY   DREAMINESS
INSPIRATION

Other rulerships:
     abstract
     actors, acting
     alcohol, alcoholic beverages

aliases
alibis
ambiguities
assassins, assassinations
astral plane
asylums
aviators, aviation
baths, bathing
bottles (containers for liquids)
cameras
chemistry, chemists, chemicals
chemical engineers, laboratories
cigarettes, cigars (tobacco products)
cinemas
clairvoyance
coffee, caffeine
con men
confidential matters
confinement, places of confinement
counterfeit, that which is
covert
dancers, dancing
drama
dreamers, dreams
drugs, drug addiction
drunkards
ecstasy, elation
E. S. P.
fear
fish, fishing
floods
fog
forgery
gas, gases
gasoline, gas stations
glass, glassware
hidden, that which is hidden from view
hospitals, hospital workers
hypnotism
illusions

imagination, one's ability to imagine
imitation
intoxication
intuition
liquids
narcotics
occult, occultism
oceans
oil, oil wells
photography, photographers, photographs
pretense, pretending
prison, prisoners, prison attendants
private investigators
prophesy, prophets
psychism, psychics, psychic experiences
sea, seamen
secrets, secret feelings, secret matters
sleep
sorrows, secret sorrows
spies
steam, steam baths
vacillation
water; any places, occupations or matters
    connected with water
witches, witchcraft
yoga, yogis

PLUTO   ♇
3,960 miles in diameter
3.7 billion miles mean distance from the sun
Time of orbit 248.4 years
20 years in each sign
Co-ruler of SCORPIO (with Mars)

Principal keywords:
  (Positive)   (Negative)
REGENERATION   COMPULSION
ELIMINATION   CRIME
THE MASSES   SUBVERSION
COOPERATION

Other rulerships:
    adulteration
    anus, rectum
    archeology, archeologists
    atomic energy: bombs, scientists
    calamities, catastrophes
    cess pools
    chasms
    coercion
    corpses
    corruption
    cremation
    crime, criminals, criminal gangs
    death, matters pertaining to the dead
    decadence
    degenerate, degeneration
    demolition
    derelicts
    dictators
    executions, executioners
    filth, foulness
    force
    gangsters
    groups, group activity
    hell
    horror, anything that is horrible
    infamy
    kidnappers, kidnapping
    legacies
    lust
    mausoleums
    monsters
    murder, homicide
    obscenity
    phoenix
    plutonium
    pollution
    pornography
    procreative act
    rackets, racketeers

```
reincarnation
rejuvenation
reproduction
reptiles
sewers
spoil, spoilage
toilets
underworld
universal welfare
venereal diseases
volcanoes
waste, that which is wasted
```

ARIES   ♈   The Ram
First sign   Cardinal Fire
Ruled by MARS
Sun in sign March 20 to April 20 (approx.)

Principal keywords:
 (Positive)   (Negative)
ASSERTIVE   AGGRESSIVE
ENERGETIC   ANGRY
COURAGEOUS   EGOTISTICAL
ARDENT   IMPULSIVE

Other rulerships:
      activity (physical)
      adventurers
      adrenal glands
      ambition
      baldness
      caps, hats
      east (direction)
      explosiveness
      eyes
      face
      fire, firemen, fire places
      force, forcefulness
      head (anything pertaining to it)
      headaches
      heat
      insomnia
      iron, steel
      leaders, leadership
      manufacturers, manufacturing
      materialism
      mechanical engineers
      military (all matters pertaining to it)
      operations, surgical
      pioneers
      temperament
      tools (primarily cutting)

TAURUS   ♉   The Bull
Second sign   Fixed Earth
Ruled by VENUS
Sun in sign April 20 to May 20

Principal keywords:
 (Positive)   (Negative)
CONSERVATIVE   GREEDY
RELIABLE   STODGY
STEADFAST   POSSESSIVE
PATIENT   OBSTINATE
DELIBERATE

Other rulerships:
     actors, actresses
     architecture
     artists
     banks, banking, bankers
     beauty, beautiful things, feeling for
       beauty
     cattle, cattlemen
     caution
     culture, cultured people
     dancers, dancing
     loans, loan companies
     money (anything pertaining to it)
     obedient
     perseverance
     possessions (one's)
     practicality
     self reliance
     singers, singing
     slow learner
     stability
     stubbornness
     thyroid gland
     trustworthiness
     vocal chords, the voice
     wheat, wheat fields

```
GEMINI     ♊     The Twins
Third sign                    Mutable Air
Ruled by MERCURY
Sun in sign May 20 to June 20

Principal keywords:
 (Positive)                    (Negative)
INTELLECTUAL                   NERVOUS
VERSATILE                      UNDEPENDABLE
COMMUNICATIVE                  IMPATIENT
ALERT                          UNABLE TO CONCENTRATE

Other rulerships:
     advertising
     arms of the body
     asthma
     bicycling
     books, bookstores
     breath, breathing
     brothers and sisters
     computers, computer operators
     cousins
     education (basic)
     handwriting
     information
     intellect, intelligence
     journalists, journalism
     journeys (short)
     lectures
     libraries
     literature, literary people
     mail, mail boxes, mail carriers
     nervous system (in general)
     printers, printing
     railroads
     relatives
     schools (lower grades)
     teachers, teaching
     writers, writings (in general)
```

CANCER   ♋   The Crab
Fourth sign   Cardinal Water
Ruled by the MOON
Sun in sign June 20 to July 20

Principal keywords:
(Positive)   (Negative)
PROTECTIVE   OVERSENSITIVE
DOMESTIC   OBLIQUE
EMOTIONAL   CRABBY
PATRIOTIC   MOODY
                               ACQUISITIVE

Other rulerships:
      agriculture
      bakers, bakeries
      baths, bathing, bathrooms
      boats, boating
      breasts, the breast
      collectors, collections
      cooks, cooking
      crying, crybabies
      digestion, digestive system
      fish, fishing, fishermen
      fluids and liquids of all sorts
      gardens, gardeners
      groceries
      home, home life
      hotels, inns
      kitchens
      laundries
      north (direction)
      nurses, nursing
      plumbers, plumbing
      restaurants, restaurant workers
      sailing, sailors
      sea, seamen, matters of the sea
      water, anything pertaining to water

LEO   ♌   The Lion
Fifth sign   Fixed Fire
Ruled by the SUN
Sun in sign July 20 to August 20

Principal keywords:
 (Positive)   (Negative)
CREATIVE   PLEASURE SEEKING
VITAL   CONCEITED
COMMANDING   DOMINEERING
EXPANSIVE   LAZY
REGAL

Other rulerships:
        amusements, places of amusement
        arrogance
        brokers
        children (in general)
        cinemas
        circuses
        creativity, ability and urge to create
        entertainment, entertainers
        gambling, gamblers, gambling places
        games of all sorts
        government, people in the government,
           government buildings
        heart
        independence
        jewels, jewelry
        kings, royalty
        motion pictures, motion picture producers
           and theatres
        parties (social)
        pleasure, all sorts
        speculations, speculators
        spine, spinal column
        sports, sporting events and stadiums
        sunny disposition
        theatres

```
VIRGO      ♍      The Virgin
Sixth sign                      Mutable Earth
Ruled by MERCURY
Sun in sign August 20 to September 20
```

Principal keywords:

(Positive)	(Negative)
PRACTICAL	RETICENT
MODEST	OVERDISCRIMINATING
ANALYTICAL	ALOOF
UNASSUMING	OVERCRITICAL

Other keywords:
```
     accounts, accounting
     administration, administrating
     animals (smaller breeds)
     charts and maps
     civil service
     clerks, clerical work
     clothing, clothing dealers
     critics, criticism
     dairies
     diet, dietitians, nutrition
     efficiency
     employment, employees
     food, food handlers, groceries
     health, care of the body
     labor, laborers
     libraries, librarians
     Navy, naval affairs and personel
     sanitation
     service, one's ability and desire to serve
     teachers, teaching
```

LIBRA   ♎   The Balance
Seventh sign   Cardinal Air
Ruled by VENUS
Sun in sign September 20 to October 20

Principal keywords:
 (Positive)   (Negative)
HARMONIOUS   INDECISIVE
AFFABLE   VAPID
DIPLOMATICAL   DISCONTENTED
BALANCED
THOUGHTFUL

Other rulerships:
     actors, actresses
     affection
     arbitration
     art, artists
     beauty, beautiful things, appreciation
        of beauty
     companionship
     compromise
     decorators
     endocrine system
     fashion
     friendship
     justice
     indecision
     kidneys
     marriage, the mate
     music, musicians, musical ability and
        appreciation
     pacificism, pacifists
     social affairs, gatherings
     symmetry
     unions
     west (direction)

SCORPIO   ♏   The Scorpion (or Eagle)
Eighth sign
Ruled by MARS and PLUTO
Sun in sign October 20 to November 20

Principal keywords:
 (Positive)   (Negative)
INTENSE   BLUNT
PASSIONATE   CRUEL
PENETRATING   LUSTFUL
GENUINE   VINDICTIVE

Other rulerships:
    butchers
    bluntness
    cess pools
    cremation, crematories
    cruelty
    death, the dead
    elimination
    executions
    feces
    funerals, mortuaries
    genitals
    hate
    insurance of all types
    legacies
    pharmacies, pharmacists
    pubic area
    rectum, anus
    regeneration, reincarnation
    reptiles
    sewers, sewage, sewage disposal
    sexual intercourse
    sorcery
    tyranny, tyrants
    urine
    venereal disease
    vice

SAGITTARIUS   ♐   The Archer
Ninth sign   Mutable Fire
Ruled by JUPITER
Sun in sign November 20 to December 20

Principal keywords:
  (Positive)   (Negative)
EXPANSIVE   RECKLESS
FREE   OUTSPOKEN
ENTHUSIASTIC   EXCESSIVE
PROFOUND   BOISTEROUS

Other rulerships:
      abundance
      aliens
      altars
      archery, archers
      arteries
      banks, banking, bankers
      ceremonies
      cheerfulness
      churches, church affairs, clergymen
      colleges, college students
      commerce
      education (higher)
      foreign affairs and countries (travel)
      hips and thighs
      horses, horsemen, races
      hunting
      journeys (long), voyages
      judges, judicial system
      law, lawyers
      philosophy, philosophers
      prayers, praying
      publishing, writings that are published
      religion, theologians
      wisdom

CAPRICORN   ♑   The Goat
Tenth sign   Cardinal Earth
Ruled by SATURN
Sun in sign December 20 to January 20

Principal keywords:
  (Positive)   (Negative)
CAUTIOUS   COLD
AMBITIOUS   LIMITED
SERIOUS   MISERLY
STABLE   FEARFUL
ORDERLY

Other rulerships:
     bones (in general)
     business, business matters
     caves
     cemeteris
     chiropractors
     clocks and watches (watchmakers)
     coal, coal mines (miners)
     cold, colds
     concentration (mental)
     conservative
     credit
     crystals, crystallization
     depression (feelings)
     farms, farming, farmers
     grain, granaries
     honors
     integrety
     land, land owners, land speculation
     leather, leather goods
     lumber, lumber yards
     mines, mining, minerals
     old people
     profession (one's)
     selling and buying
     time, timekeepers

AQUARIUS   ♒   The Water Bearer
Eleventh sign   Fixed Air
Ruled by SATURN and URANUS
Sun in sign January 20 to February 20

Principal keywords:
  (Positive)   (Negative)
INSTRUCTIVE   REVOLUTIONARY
INVENTIVE   DETACHED
ASPIRING   COOL
CHANGEABLE   REBELLIOUS
UNCONVENTIONAL

Other rulerships:
    acquaintances
    airplanes, airplane workers, airports
    altruism, altruists
    astrology, astrologers
    aviation, aviators
    electricity, electricians, electric
      products
    electronics, electronic technicians
    friends, friendliness
    inventions, inventors, one's ability
      to invent
    modern or new, anything that is
    motors
    photography, photographers, photographic
      supplies
    psychology, psychiatry
    radio and television, anything pertaining
      to it
    rebellions and revolutions
    reforms, reformers
    science
    social affairs, social functions
    socialism (political)
    societies in general
    X-ray, X-ray technicians

PISCES   ♓   The Fishes
Twelfth sign
Ruled by JUPITER and NEPTUNE
Sun in sign February 20 to March 20

Principal keywords:
  (Positive)   (Negative)
INTUITIVE   VAGUE
INSPIRED   OVERSENTIMENTAL
SENSITIVE   CONFUSED
INTANGIBLE   SELF-PITYING

Other rulerships:
      abstract
      alcohol, alcoholic beverages, alcoholism
      anesthetics
      asylums
      bartenders
      charity, charitable institutions
      cheats, cheating
      clairvoyance
      clouds, fog
      confinement, place of confinement
      conspiracies
      disappointments
      divers, diving
      drugs
      enemies, secret
      fish, fishing, fishermen
      gas (appliances)
      gasoline, gasoline station
      hospitals
      imprisonment
      institutions of all kinds
      lymph, lymphatic system
      mediums (spirit)
      Navy, naval affairs and personel
      occult, occultists, one's occult abilities
      oceans, oceanographer
      oil, oilwells

photography, photographers, photographic
   equipment
poisons, poisoning
poor, poor people, poverty
pretenses, pretenders
psychics, psychism
secrets, secret matters
ships, shipping
shoes, shoe dealers
sleep
sorrows
suffering
swimmers, swimming
water, anyting pertaining to water

FIRST HOUSE
Natural sign ruler: ARIES
Natural planet ruler: MARS

Principal significance:
     THE BODY AND INHERENT HEALTH OF THE NATIVE;
     HIS PHYSICAL APPEARANCE AND CONDITION;
     HIS PERSONALITY

Other rulerships:
     abnormalities, one's physical
     actions, one's
     attitudes, one's
     birth, one's
     change of one's location
     characteristics, one's
     dawn, sunrise
     desire, one's
     disposition, one's
     environment, early
     eyes, one's
     face, one's
     habits
     head
     life, length of
     mannerisms, one's
     outlook on life
     personal affairs
     self, self interest
     temperament

SECOND HOUSE
Natural sign ruler: TAURUS
Natural planet ruler: VENUS

Principal significance:
     POSSESSIONS; MONEY; GAIN AND LOSSES

Other rulerships:
     assets
     banks, bankers, banking
     bank account, one's
     budgets
     cashiers
     checkbooks, checks
     debts, one's own
     earning capacity
     earnings
     ears
     financial condition, one's
     giving and receiving
     incomes
     interest
     investors, investments
     neck
     ownership
     prices
     profit
     purchasing power
     resources, one's
     safes, strongboxes
     securities
     stocks and bonds
     stockbrokers, stock exchanges
     throat
     travelers's checks
     wealth

THIRD HOUSE
Natural sign ruler: GEMINI
Natural planet ruler: MERCURY

Principal significance:
    COMMUNICATION BY ANY MEANS; BROTHERS
    AND SISTERS; SHORT JOURNEYS; NEIGHBORS

Other rulerships:
    adaptability
    arms, hands and shoulders
    books, bookstores
    bookkeepers, bookkeeping
    breath, breathing
    cleverness
    commuting
    concentrate, ability to
    contracts
    correspondence
    debates
    education, lower
    gossip
    ideas
    information, informants
    intelligence, intellect
    lectures, lecturing, lecturers
    letters, letter writing
    libraries, librarians
    lungs
    memory
    nerves, the nervous system
    news, newspapers, the press
    periodicals
    rumors
    speech, speaking
    telephones
    travel, short range
    writers, writing

FOURTH HOUSE
Natural sign ruler: CANCER
Natural planet ruler: MOON

Principal significance:
     THE HOME; FATHER (OR MOTHER); LAND;
     BEGINNING AND END OF LIFE

Other rulerships:
     birthplace, one's
     breasts
     buildings, public buildings
     chest (of the body)
     crops
     digestion, digestive organs
     domestic life and environment
     environment late in life
     estates
     family, one's
     farms, farming, farmers
     gardens, gardeners
     graves, grave stones
     hotels, motels
     illness, terminal
     mines, mining, miners
     old age
     old people
     outcome
     real estate, realtors
     wombs

```
FIFTH HOUSE
Natural sign ruler:  LEO
Natural planet ruler:  SUN

Principal significance:
     CREATIONS (CHILDREN); PLEASURES (INCLUDING
     SEXUAL); GAMBLING AND SPECULATION

Other rulerships:
     amusements, amusement places
     artistic endeavers
     baths, bathing
     bets, betting
     casinos
     chance, the laws of
     cinemas
     circuses
     concerts, concert halls
     courtships
     creativity, creative ability
     entertainers, place of entertainment
     games
     heart
     love affairs, lovers
     motion pictures, motion picture theatres
     parenthood
     parties (social)
     procreation
     recreation
     resorts
     romance
     sexual intercourse
     speculation
     sports
     stockbrokers, stock exchanges
     theatres
     vacations
```

SIXTH HOUSE
Natural sign ruler: VIRGO
Natural planet ruler: MERCURY

Principal significance:
    WORK (THE JOB); CO-WORKERS OR EMPLOYEES;
    HEALTH (AS ACQUIRED OR MAINTAINED)

Other rulerships:
    animals, small or domestic
    Army, army matters
    body, care of
    bowels
    civil service
    cleaners
    clothing
    comforts
    cooks, cooking
    craftsmen, craftmanship
    disease in general
    doctors
    dogs
    food, food workers
    humane societies
    hygiene, hygienics
    injuries caused by animals
    intestines
    labor, laborers
    medical profession
    military services
    Navy, naval matters
    nurse, nursing
    nutrition
    pets, pet shops
    physicians
    police
    poultry, poultry farmers
    restaurants, restaurant workers
    sanitation, sanitation workers
    service
    servants
    tenants

```
SEVENTH HOUSE
Natural sign ruler:  LIBRA
Natural planet ruler:  VENUS

Principal significance:
     THE MATE; A PARTNER; OPPONENTS, RIVALS OR
     OPEN ENEMIES

Other rulerships:
     alliances
     business partners
     contests
     contracts
     divorce
     duels
     fiances
     fugitives
     husband
     kidneys
     lawsuits
     love, lovers
     marriage
     nephews and nieces
     ovaries
     public, one's dealings with
     public enemies
     spouse
     sunset
     veins
     wife
```

EIGHTH HOUSE
Natural sign ruler: SCORPIO
Natural planet rulers: MARS and PLUTO

Principal significance:
     OTHER PEOPLE'S MONEY; DEATH

Other rulerships:
     alimony
     autopsies
     bankruptcy
     bladder
     coroners
     dead, anything pertaining to the dead
     debts, debtors
     dowries
     executions, executioners
     genitals
     graveyards
     heirs
     inheritances
     insurance, insurance companies
     legacies
     life after death
     money owed to one
     money of the dead
     morticians
     occultism, occultists
     rebirth
     regeneration
     reincarnation
     suicides
     taxes, taxation
     venereal diseases
     wills

NINTH HOUSE
Natural sign ruler: SAGITTARIUS
Natural planet ruler: JUPITER

Principal significance:
    HIGHER LEARNING; LONG JOURNEYS; RELIGION
    AND PHILOSOPHY; PUBLISHING

Other rulerships:
    advertising
    aliens
    attorneys
    churches, church affairs
    clergymen
    colleges, college students
    commerce
    courts of law
    foreign countries, people, travel
    hips and thighs
    ideals, one's
    imports-exports
    in-laws, one's
    legal profession
    legal affairs
    litigation
    liver
    metaphysics
    philanthropy, philanthropists
    philosophers
    prayer, praying
    publications
    rituals
    science in general
    ships, shippers, shipping
    spirituality, spiritual happenings
    theologians

TENTH HOUSE
Natural sign ruler: CAPRICORN
Natural planet ruler: SATURN

Principal significance:
    THE CAREER, HONORS; MOTHER (OR FATHER)

Other rulerships:
    achievement
    advancement
    authority, one's own
    bones
    bosses
    community standing, one's
    credit, one's
    dignity
    employers
    employment, one's
    esteem
    executives, executive ability
    fame
    goals, one's
    kings
    knees
    notoriety
    people, famous or important
    popularity
    praise that is received
    presidents
    prestige
    profession, one's
    professional men
    promotions
    public standing or appearance, one's
    reputation
    superiors, one's
    vocations

ELEVENTH HOUSE
Natural sign ruler: AQUARIUS
Natural planet rulers: SATURN and URANUS

Principal significance:
     FRIENDS; HOPES AND WISHES

Other rulerships:
     acquaintances
     ankles
     aspirations
     associates
     calves (of the legs)
     civic organizations
     clubs, club members, club houses
     companions
     cooperation
     desires, one's
     fraternities
     legs, lower
     memberships
     objectives
     organizations
     societies in general
     sororities

TWELFTH HOUSE
Natural sign ruler: PISCES
Natural planet rulers: JUPITER and NEPTUNE

Principal significance:
     SORROWS; CONFINEMENT; INSTITUTIONS; SECRET
     ENEMIES; SELF UNDOING

Other rulerships:
     afflicitions
     anxieties
     assassins, assassinations
     asylums
     blackmail
     bondage
     bribes, bribery
     charity, charitable institutions
     cheaters, cheating
     conspiracies
     crime, criminals
     deception, deceivers
     disappointments
     drugs, drug addiction
     escape
     falsehoods and lies
     fear
     feet
     forgers, forgeries
     fraud
     grief
     handicaps
     hospitals, hospital workers
     karma
     limitations
     loneliness
     losses
     meditation
     oil, oil wells
     pain
     poverty

prison, prisoners, prison workers
psychism, psychics, psychic abilities
retirement
scandal
secrets, secret societies
sleep
subversion
suicides
welfare, welfare workers
worry

PLANETARY DAYS OF THE WEEK

Moon	Monday
Mars	Tuesday
Mercury	Wednesday
Jupiter	Thursday
Venus	Friday
Saturn	Saturday
Sun	Sunday

METALS ASSIGNED TO THE PLANETS

Sun	gold
Moon	silver
Mercury	mercury
Venus	copper
Mars	iron
Jupiter	tin
Saturn	lead
Uranus	uranium
Neptune	neptunium
Pluto	plutonium

MAJOR AREAS OF THE BODY RULED BY THE SIGNS

Aries	head (face)
Taurus	neck and throat
Gemini	arms and lungs and nervous system
Cancer	chest, breasts and stomach
Leo	heart and back
Virgo	solar plexus and bowels
Libra	kidneys and loins
Scorpio	sex organs
Sagittarius	hips and thighs
Capricorn	knees
Aquarius	calves and ankles
Pisces	feet

THE BOOK SHOP

CHART PACK   (Postpaid)   1.00
Contains five each of the following: the regular chart form (Appendix P), the 360° chart form (Appendix Q), the planets work sheet,
and the houses work sheet (as used in the text).
25 of any one of the above   (Postpaid)   1.00

ASPECT FINDER OVERLAYS   (Postpaid)   2.95
These overlays differ radically from the usually inaccurate machine-
made cardboard wheels. They are designed to be used with the 360°
chart; a map pin through the center provides precise alignment.
Eliminates much of the tedious work in finding the aspects in any
chart. Pack includes set of two clear acetate overlays, map pin, ten
charts, and complete instruction for use.

Send orders to:

URANUS PUBLISHING CO.
5050 Calatrana Drive
Woodland Hills, Calif. 91364

Be sure to PRINT your name and address and include your ZIP number.

(Note: For ephemerides, tables of houses, and other astrological books, check
with the store or mail order company from which you purchased your basics.
If they are unable to supply your needs, please contact us & ask for our catalog.)